W0081461

SIMPLY
DELICIOUS

100+ Quick and **Easy Recipes**
Made with **Time-Saving
Techniques**—Slow Cooker,
Sheet Pan, Air Fryer,
One Pot, and More

KYNDRA **HOLLEY**

VICTORY BELT PUBLISHING INC.

LAS VEGAS

First published in 2025 by Victory Belt Publishing Inc.

Copyright © 2025 Kyndra Holley

No part of this publication may be reproduced or distributed in any form or by any means, electronic or mechanical, or stored in a database or retrieval system, without prior written permission from the publisher.

ISBN-13: 978-1-628605-71-6

The author is not a licensed practitioner, physician, or medical professional and offers no medical diagnoses, treatments, suggestions, or counseling. The information presented herein has not been evaluated by the U.S. Food and Drug Administration, and it is not intended to diagnose, treat, cure, or prevent any disease. Full medical clearance from a licensed physician should be obtained before beginning or modifying any diet, exercise, or lifestyle program, and physicians should be informed of all nutritional changes.

The author/owner claims no responsibility to any person or entity for any liability, loss, or damage caused or alleged to be caused directly or indirectly as a result of the use, application, or interpretation of the information presented herein.

Cover and interior design by Yordan Terziev, Boryana Yordanova, and Kat Lannom

Illustrations by Elita San Juan

Recipe photos by Jo Harding

Printed in Canada

TC 0125

To the incredible group of strangers-turned-friends who restored my faith in humanity and became my lifeline when I needed it most: my Gram Fam.

Most of you I have never met in person, but your kindness, support, and unwavering belief in me pulled me through the darkest chapter of my life. Your constant messages of love and support, cards, letters, gifts, and your mere presence in my life, even if only online, made more of a difference than I could ever articulate. This book is as much yours as it is mine, and I dedicate it to each of you—for showing up for me when I needed it most.

Thank you for saving me.

One more thing… Thank you for helping me reclaim Christmas.

K, Love You, Bye!

Kyndra (and Chewy and Ollie)

CONTENTS

ABOUT THIS BOOK

Welcome to *Simply Delicious*—your go-to guide for preparing mouthwatering meals that are as simple as they are satisfying. This cookbook is all about helping you create delicious dishes without a lot of stress and mess. Whether you're a seasoned cook or a novice in the kitchen, this book is loaded with recipes that are approachable and easy to bring to life, but never compromise on flavor.

Each chapter offers a different approach to cooking (sheet pan cooking, one-pot meals, slow cooker recipes, toasts, boards and bowls, etc.), so you can mix things up based on your mood, your schedule, or the ingredients you have on hand. From 30-minute meals to one-pot wonders to slow cooker and air fryer cooking to using up leftovers, *Simply Delicious* has something for every taste and every occasion.

Here's a peek at what you'll find:

- **Sheet Pan Recipes:** Wholesome, hearty dishes with minimal cleanup

- **30-Minute Recipes:** Fast and flavorful recipes perfect for busy nights

- **One-Pot Wonders:** Simple, all-in-one dishes that are ideal for busy weeknights

- **From the Slow Cooker:** Set-it-and-forget-it meals that are rich in flavor

- **Boards and Bowls:** Creative and inspired ways to serve meals that everyone will enjoy

- **Toasts:** Delicious sweet and savory toast recipes to elevate your bread game

- **From the Air Fryer:** Quick, satisfying meals with a lighter twist

- **Casseroles and Pastas:** Cozy, comforting meals for feeding family and friends

- **Homemade Basics:** Essential staples to complement the recipes throughout the book

- **Repurposing Leftovers:** Last night's dinner transformed into something new and exciting

In the back of the book, you will even find an allergen and dietary preference index noting which recipes are gluten free, dairy free, egg free, nut free, vegetarian, and low carb, along with a traditional word-by-word index.

MASTERING MEAL PREP

Meal prep is a game-changer for anyone looking to free up time during the week, reduce stress around mealtimes, or make healthier food choices. Whether your goal is to prep just ingredients or entire meals, dedicating one day each week to meal prep can free up a lot of time in the long run. No more scrambling to throw something together at the last minute or relying on takeout; instead, you can enjoy fresh, homemade meals that are ready to eat whenever you want them.

In this section, I cover different meal prep techniques, offer tips and tricks for success, and guide you through planning and preparing meals that will keep you fueled and satisfied. In the "Meal Plans and Prep" section (page 15), I offer seven different meal plans, including options for breakfast only, breakfast and lunch, and dinner only, to fit a variety of lifestyles and needs.

WHAT IS MEAL PREP?

Meal prep is the process of planning, preparing, and storing recipe components or meals ahead of time. This can mean cooking entire meals or simply prepping ingredients like vegetables and proteins for quick cooking or assembling later. The key to meal prep success is organization. Whether you're preparing a week of work lunches, family dinners, or grab-and-go breakfasts, having a plan will get you in and out of the kitchen much faster.

BENEFITS OF MEAL PREP

Meal planning and meal prep are the ultimate kitchen time-savers, transforming the way you cook, eat, and shop. By setting aside a little time each week to plan meals and prepare ingredients in advance, you'll cut down on last-minute stress, reduce food waste, and make healthier choices effortlessly. Whether you're aiming to save money, eat more balanced meals, or simply make dinnertime easier, having a plan in place ensures you're never left scrambling for what's next. Plus, prepping ahead means less cleanup during the week—because who doesn't love a smoother, stress-free mealtime?

- **Saves time:** Prepping meals or ingredients in bulk reduces time spent in the kitchen, freeing you up for more fun activities.

- **Lessens decision fatigue:** Knowing what you're going to eat eliminates the dreaded nightly question: "What's for dinner?"

- **Encourages better eating habits:** Planning meals in advance can help you stick to healthier choices and prevent last-minute stops for fast food out of convenience.

- **Limits food waste:** When you plan meals and prep ingredients, you're less likely to let fresh food go bad, as you are shopping with intention and have a plan for each ingredient you purchase.

- **Saves money:** Batch cooking, shopping sales, and buying ingredients that will be used across multiple meals can help reduce your overall grocery budget. (See also "10 Tips for Budget Grocery Shopping," page 46.)

MEAL PREP LIKE A PRO

Meal prep doesn't have to be complicated or time-consuming—it's all about finding a system that works for you. Whether you're prepping full meals, batch-cooking ingredients, or simply chopping veggies in advance, a little planning goes a long way in making your week easier, healthier, and more budget-friendly. By mapping out your meals, shopping strategically, and storing everything properly, you'll set yourself up for effortless breakfasts, stress-free lunches, and quick, satisfying dinners. This step-by-step guide will help you master meal prep so you can spend less time cooking and more time enjoying your food.

STEP 1 MAP OUT YOUR MEALS

- **Pick a meal-prep day:** Dedicate one day each week (I typically choose Sunday) to planning and preparing.

- **Choose your meals:** Start by looking at your schedule. How many breakfasts, lunches, dinners, and/or snacks will you need? Are you only needing quick breakfasts for work mornings? Do you work long days and need to pack both breakfast and lunch, but can cook dinner at home? Figure out what kind of meals you will make, taking into account meals you'll eat out so that you don't end up prepping more food than you can reasonably eat.

- **Pick recipes that are meal-prep friendly:** You want to ensure that you are making dishes that will actually taste good when reheated, or else what is the point? Look for dishes that store well and are easy to warm up, such as casseroles, stir-fries, protein bowls, soups, and slow cooker recipes.

- **Plan enough variety:** I personally can eat the same dish over and over without getting tired of it. But if you are someone who needs a lot of variety to avoid food fatigue, make sure to pick recipes that include different proteins, vegetables, and flavors to enjoy throughout the week. That being said, if you don't mind a little repetition, you can save a lot of time and money by utilizing the same ingredients across multiple dishes. As an example: Think of all the different ways you can prepare chicken or use roasted vegetables throughout meals.

- **Balance nutrients:** Make sure that the meals you choose complement each other in terms of balancing protein, healthy fats, carbohydrates, and fiber.

STEP 2 MAKE A SHOPPING LIST

- **Take inventory:** Check your fridge, freezer, and pantry and take note of what you already have on hand to avoid buying duplicates.

- **Get organized:** Create a list based on categories—produce, pantry, protein, dairy, etc.—with the layout of your usual grocery store in mind. This will help when you shop, as the categories will align with the layout of the grocery store.

- **Be mindful of budget:** Once you have your list, stick to it and avoid impulse buys and overconsumption. (See "10 Tips for Budget Grocery Shopping," page 46.)

STEP 3 EXECUTE YOUR MEAL PREP

There is no right or wrong way to meal prep. It's all about finding what works best for you. It does not have to be an all-or-nothing endeavor. Here are two efficient meal-prep strategies:

- **Ingredient prep:** This includes cutting up all of the vegetables for the recipes you chose; prepping and/or marinating proteins; hard-boiling eggs; cooking rice; and making dips, dressings, and sauces—basically, anything that will allow you to cut down on cook time throughout the week. Many people exclusively meal prep this way, especially if simply making dinnertime more efficient is the goal.

- **Batch cooking:** Another form of meal prep is preparing and cooking large batches of proteins, vegetables, starches, snacks, etc., and then combining them throughout the week to make quick and easy meals. The grill is a great tool here as you can grill all your proteins outside while cooking the vegetables and starches inside. If I have a protein prepped, along with large batches of vegetables and starches, I can turn them into a hundred different meals.

Batch cooking can also mean fully executing recipes, portioning them out into individual servings, and then refrigerating or freezing as necessary.

STEP 4: PORTION, LABEL, AND STORE

Proper storage is key to keeping prepped meals fresh and making sure they still taste great when you go to reheat them.

- **Portion:** You can portion each recipe into single-serve containers for easy grab-and-go breakfasts and lunches, or you can pack full meals into larger containers to pull out after a long day for a ready-made dinner for the family. I recommend using glass containers with airtight lids, opposed to plastic. It's healthier for both storage and reheating. If batch-cooking ingredients (not full recipes), store cooked proteins, vegetables, and starches separately.

- **Label:** Use a simple labeling system, such as masking tape or dissolvable labels, to note the name of the meal and prep date.

- **Store:** Most prepped meals will keep for three to five days in the fridge when stored in airtight containers. Freezing extends their life to several months. Great candidates for freezing include soups, stews, chilis, and casseroles. Use freezer-safe containers or bags, and label everything with the name of the dish, as well as the date.

REHEAT AND EAT

Now that your meals are prepped, all that's left is reheating and enjoying them!

TIPS AND TRICKS FOR SUCCESSFUL MEAL PREP

- **Start small:** Begin by prepping just a few meals or snacks each week. As you get comfortable, you can increase the number.

- **Keep a list of go-to recipes:** Create a meal-prep rotation with recipes you know and love, making planning easier.

- **Mix and match:** Prep individual components (proteins, vegetables, and starches) that you can combine in different ways throughout the week for variety.

- **Make Freezer Meals:** Batch-cooking freezer-friendly meals like chili or lasagna saves time in future weeks. Same goes for making a double batch of whatever you are prepping. Use half that week and freeze half to save time later.

- **Invest in quality containers:** Good storage containers will keep food fresh longer and make reheating more efficient.

STORAGE IDEAS FOR MEAL PREP

- **Glass containers with lids:** Perfect for storing prepped ingredients and meals, as they are durable, microwave-safe, and eco-friendly. Choose stackable options to maximize fridge and freezer space.

- **Portion-control containers:** Use containers with multiple compartments to keep proteins, vegetables, and starches separate for individual lunches or dinners and to maintain reasonable portion sizes.

- **Bento boxes:** A stylish and functional option for meal-prepped lunches or snacks with multiple compartments for different foods.

- **Freezer-safe containers:** Freeze soups, stews, casseroles, or chili in individual portions for future use.

- **Mason jars:** Ideal for salads, overnight oats, smoothies, and layered meals that you can grab and go. Store premeasured dry grains and spices in jars to reduce clutter and ensure quick access. This is also a great opportunity to upcycle jars from things like sauces, pickles, and condiments.

- **Reusable silicone bags:** Great for portioning out snacks, storing precut fruits and vegetables, and freezing cooked proteins.

- **Vacuum-seal bags:** Perfect for sauces, soups, stews, and other liquid-y foods.

- **Silicone muffin molds:** For easy reheating, use silicone molds to portion and freeze sauces, pesto, or cooked eggs and then transfer to freezer bags.

TIPS FOR KEEPING INGREDIENTS FRESH

- **Use airtight containers:** Store prepped ingredients in airtight glass containers to prevent moisture and air from spoiling the food.

- **Label and date everything:** Write the preparation date and the contents on containers and bags so there's no mystery food and you'll know how long each item has been stored.

- **Separate ethylene-producing fruits:** Keep fruits like apples and bananas (which emit ethylene gas and can speed up ripening) separate from more sensitive produce, like leafy greens.

- **Line containers for chopped fruits and vegetables with paper towels:** Keep prepped vegetables like carrots, celery, onions, and even salad greens in paper towel–lined containers in the fridge to absorb excess moisture. Replace the paper towels with fresh ones every couple of days. Alternatively, you can store things like prepped carrots and celery upright in a jar of water in the fridge. This will help them retain their freshness and crunch.

- **Store fresh herbs upright in water:** Fresh herbs like cilantro and parsley are best when kept upright in a jar in about 2 inches of water. They will last three times as long.

- **Don't wash produce until ready to use:** For more delicate fruits and vegetables, that are more easily prone to spoilage, like berries and lettuce, wait until just before use to wash them to avoid adding extra moisture that can cause them to spoil faster.

- **Vacuum seal for longer storage:** Use vacuum-seal bags or machines to remove excess air from containers, which helps keep proteins, grains, and vegetables fresh longer in the fridge. This can also help save space when freezing extra ingredients or leftovers, as the vacuum-sealed packages can lie flat and are easily stackable.

- **Freeze excess ingredients:** If you won't use prepped ingredients within 3 to 5 days, freeze them in portions to preserve freshness and prevent spoilage.

- **Blanch and freeze vegetables:** Briefly boil (blanch) vegetables like broccoli, green beans, and carrots before freezing to preserve their color, texture, and nutrients.

- **Rotate prepped foods:** Follow the "first in, first out" rule, using older prepped ingredients before newer ones to reduce food waste and ensure that nothing spoils

Sausage, Egg & Cheese
8/2

Bacon, Egg & Cheese
8/2

MEAL PLANS AND PREP

I wanted to tackle the meal plans in this book a little differently than I have in my past cookbooks. After years and years of doing meal prep, I've come to realize that most meal plans are severely lacking when it comes to guidance and direction. Sure, they give you a list of recipes to make for the week, but they never tell you how to execute the plan as efficiently as possible.

I believe the meal plans that follow are a considerably less intimidating, more efficient, and more informative way to tackle meal planning and meal prep. They are also more realistic in that they provide a variety of solutions for different schedules and lifestyles. Not everyone needs a seven-day meal plan that feeds four people breakfast, lunch, dinner, and a snack. Not to mention that trying to meal prep that many meals all in one day feels impossible.

It's more likely that you might need quick grab-and-go breakfasts Monday through Friday. Or your workday is so demanding that you need to pack breakfast and lunch but do have time to cook dinner in the evening. Conversely, maybe you have no problem getting in a nourishing breakfast and lunch, but by the time you get home, you are far too tired to even think about cooking and just want a quick and easy dinner that you can simply heat and eat.

These seven meal plans (three breakfast-only, two breakfast and lunch, and two dinner-only) will teach you the steps and tools needed to take any of the recipes in this book, plug them into this format, and end up with ready-to-eat meals that will feed you throughout the week. For example, in the first meal plan, you'll see that prepping the casserole for the oven while the egg bites steam makes for efficient multitasking. While recipes are cooking or baking, you're free for cleanup. You're out of the kitchen in just under two hours with a week's worth of breakfasts ready to go!

BREAKFAST-ONLY
WEEKLY MEAL PREP PLAN

122

Bacon and Gruyère Egg Bites

281

French Toast Casserole

Total servings: 11

- 5 servings of Bacon and Gruyère Egg Bites (2 egg bites per serving)
- 6 servings of French Toast Casserole

Total active time (prep work, assembly, cleanup): 45 minutes

Total hands-off time: 1 hour 45 minutes

Total meal prep time: 2 hours 30 minutes

TIME-SAVING SHORTCUTS

Swapping in some conveniently pre-prepped ingredients will save you some time—if there is room in the budget, of course.

- *Buy precooked bacon or chopped cooked bacon.*
- *Buy shredded bag cheese.*
- *Buy washed and sliced strawberries.*

SHOPPING LIST

Don't forget to check your fridge, freezer, and pantry to take inventory of what you already have on hand and cross-reference it with the grocery list. You likely have many of the pantry ingredients you'll need for these recipes.

PRODUCE

- Strawberries

DAIRY AND EGGS

- Butter
- Cottage cheese, 1 (8-ounce) container
- Eggs, 12
- Gruyère cheese, 1 small block
- Milk, 1¾ cups
- Parmesan cheese, 1 small block
- Whipped cream (or heavy cream)

MEAT

- Bacon

PANTRY

- Brioche buns, 8
- Brown sugar
- Cinnamon
- Cornstarch
- Hot sauce
- Maple syrup
- Nutmeg
- Pecans
- Tapioca starch
- Vanilla bean paste
- White vinegar

GAME PLAN

Step 1: Gather Ingredients and Equipment

Bacon and Gruyère Egg Bites: blender, silicone egg bite mold with lid, Dutch oven (or large high-sided skillet with lid)

French Toast Casserole: 9- by 13-inch baking dish, whisk, large mixing bowl, foil, small bowl

Step 2: Prepare Bacon and Brioche

1. Cook and finely chop the bacon for the egg bites.

2. Cube the stale brioche buns for the French Toast Casserole.

Step 3: Assemble Egg Bites

1. Blend the egg bite mixture as directed.

2. Add the bacon and cheese to the molds.

3. Fill the molds with the egg mixture.

> **Efficiency Tip:** *While blending and assembling, start boiling the water for the water bath.*

Step 4: Cook Egg Bites

Place the mold in the Dutch oven, add water, bring to a boil, and steam for 12 to 15 minutes.

> **Efficiency Tip:** *While the egg bites steam, move on to Step 5.*

Step 5: Assemble Casserole

1. Whisk together the custard.

2. Toss the brioche cubes in the custard mixture and let soak for 1 hour.

3. Pour the mixture into the greased baking dish.

4. Drizzle with the butter-sugar mixture and add the pecans.

Step 6: Bake Casserole

Cover the casserole with foil and bake for 30 minutes, then uncover and bake for 15 more minutes.

> **Efficiency Tip:** *Clean up the blender, bowls, and pans while the casserole finishes baking.*

Step 7: Cool and Store

Bacon and Gruyère Egg Bites: Remove from the mold and let cool. Portion into meal prep containers, 2 egg bites per serving.

French Toast Casserole: After cooling, portion into meal prep containers.

STORAGE AND REHEATING

Bacon and Gruyère Egg Bites:

- Store in the fridge for up to 5 days. Freeze any leftovers.

- Reheat in the microwave for 1 to 2 minutes or in the air fryer at 350°F for 5 minutes.

French Toast Casserole:

- Store in the fridge for up to 5 days. Freeze any leftovers.

- Reheat in the microwave for 2 minutes or in the oven at 350°F for 10 to 15 minutes.

BREAKFAST-ONLY
WEEKLY MEAL PREP PLAN

278

Ham and Cheese Croissant Casserole

124

Baked Ham and Egg Skillet

Total servings: 10

- 6 servings of Ham and Cheese Croissant Casserole
- 4 servings of Baked Ham and Egg Skillet

Total active time (prep work, assembly, cleanup): 50 minutes

Total hands-off time: 1 hour (Both recipes are cooking or baking during this time, freeing you up for cleanup.)

Total meal prep time: 1 hour 50 minutes

TIME-SAVING SHORTCUTS

- *Buy shredded cheese.*
- *Buy cleaned and sliced leeks.*
- *Substitute dried herbs for fresh.*

SHOPPING LIST

Don't forget to check your fridge, freezer, and pantry to take inventory of what you already have on hand and cross-reference with the grocery list.

PRODUCE

- Fresh basil
- Fresh chives
- Fresh thyme
- Leek, 1 small

DAIRY AND EGGS

- Butter, 1 stick
- Crumbled goat cheese, 1 small container
- Eggs, 13
- Gruyère cheese, 1 small block
- Half-and-half, 2 cups
- Heavy cream, ½ cup
- Sharp white cheddar cheese, 1 small block
- Sour cream, ⅔ cup

MEAT

- Black Forest ham, 10 ounces
- Cooked ham steak

PANTRY

- Croissants, 10
- Dijon mustard
- Dried minced onion
- Everything bagel seasoning (or make Herby Everything Seasoning, page 314)
- Garlic powder
- Pesto

GAME PLAN

Step 1: Gather Ingredients and Equipment

Ham and Cheese Croissant Casserole: 9- by 13-inch baking dish, whisk, mixing bowls, foil

Baked Ham and Egg Skillet: ovenproof skillet, ramekins, whisk, wooden spoon

Step 2: Assemble Casserole

1. Make the egg mixture: Whisk together the eggs, half-and-half, half of the Gruyère, half of the cheddar, the sour cream, Dijon mustard, chives, dried minced onion, thyme, salt, garlic powder, and pepper until well combined.

2. Arrange the croissants: Place the croissant pieces in the greased baking dish and pour the egg mixture over the croissants. Toss to coat and refrigerate for 30 minutes.

Step 3: Sauté Ham and Leeks

In a large skillet, melt the butter over medium heat and cook the ham and leeks until softened and golden. Set aside.

> **Tip:** If you're using a different protein or veggie (like mushrooms or spinach), prep it now.

Step 4: Assemble and Cook Skillet

1. Make the sauce: In the same skillet, whisk together the heavy cream, sour cream, pesto, and salt. Bring to a boil over medium-low heat, then turn off the heat.

2. Add the cheese: Stir in the Gruyère and add most of the cooked ham and leeks, reserving some for garnish.

3. Crack the eggs: Crack each egg into a ramekin and gently slide them into the creamy sauce. Transfer the skillet to the oven and bake at 400°F for 10 to 12 minutes, until the eggs are cooked to your liking.

Step 5: Finish Casserole

1. Add the ham and cheese: After refrigerating the casserole for 30 minutes, tuck the ham slices between the croissants. Top with the remaining cheese.

2. Cover with foil and bake at 350°F for 30 minutes. Uncover and bake for an additional 15 to 20 minutes, until the casserole is golden brown and the croissants are crispy.

Step 6: Garnish, Cool, and Store

Ham and Cheese Croissant Casserole:
Garnish with extra chives, thyme, and everything bagel seasoning.

Baked Ham and Egg Skillet: Top with the reserved ham, leeks, goat cheese, basil, and black pepper.

Let both recipes cool slightly before portioning into meal prep containers.

STORAGE AND REHEATING

Ham and Cheese Croissant Casserole:

- Store in the fridge for up to 5 days. Freeze any leftovers.

- Reheat in the microwave for 2 to 3 minutes or in the oven at 350°F for 10 to 15 minutes.

Baked Ham and Egg Skillet:

- Store in the fridge for up to 4 days. Freeze any leftovers.

- Reheat in the microwave for 1 to 2 minutes or in a skillet over medium-low heat until warmed through.

BREAKFAST-ONLY
WEEKLY MEAL PREP PLAN

127

Freezer Breakfast Sandwiches

277

Biscuits and Gravy Casserole

Total servings: 16

- 12 Freezer Breakfast Sandwiches
- 4 servings of Biscuits and Gravy Casserole

Total active time (prep work, assembly, cleanup): 40 minutes

Total hands-off time: 55 minutes (Both recipes are cooking or baking during this time, freeing you up for cleanup.)

Total meal prep time: 1 hour 35 minutes

TIME-SAVING SHORTCUTS

- *Buy precooked bacon.*

- *Make all 12 sandwiches the same instead of making 3 different varieties. This is both a time-saver and a money-saver.*

SHOPPING LIST

Don't forget to check your fridge, freezer, and pantry to take inventory of what you already have on hand and cross-reference it with the grocery list.

PRODUCE

- Fresh chives
- Yellow onion, 1 small

MEAT

- Bacon, 8 slices
- Canadian bacon or ham, 8 slices
- Cooked sausage patties (English muffin size), 4
- Ground pork sausage, 1 pound

DAIRY AND EGGS

- American cheese, 4 slices
- Butter, 6 tablespoons
- Cheddar cheese, 1 small block
- Cottage cheese, 1 (8-ounce) container
- Eggs, 12
- Milk, 3 cups
- Pepper jack cheese, 1 small block
- Refrigerated biscuit dough, 1 (16-ounce) can
- Swiss cheese, 1 small block
- White cheddar cheese, 1 small block

PANTRY

- All-purpose flour
- English muffins, 12
- Everything bagel seasoning (or make Herby Everything Seasoning, page 314)
- Garlic powder
- Onion powder

GAME PLAN

Step 1: Gather Ingredients and Equipment

Freezer Breakfast Sandwiches: silicone muffin top pan (for cooking eggs), parchment paper, foil, Sharpie (for labeling), large mixing bowls

Biscuits and Gravy Casserole: ovenproof skillet, whisk, mixing bowls, foil

Step 2: Prepare for Casserole and Sandwiches

1. Casserole prep: Preheat the oven to 350°F.

2. Sandwich prep: Toast the English muffins, cook the sausage and bacon, and warm the ham.

Step 3: Prepare Eggs for Sandwiches

In a blender, combine the eggs, cottage cheese, and seasoning. Pulse until smooth. Pour the mixture into the muffin top pan, dividing it evenly between the 12 wells.

Step 4: Cook Eggs for Sandwiches

Place the muffin pan in the oven and bake the eggs for 15 minutes, or until cooked through and soft with a spongy texture.

> **Efficiency Tip:** *While the eggs are baking, move on to Step 5.*

Step 5: Make Gravy for Casserole

1. Melt 1 tablespoon of butter in a large skillet over medium heat. Add the sausage and cook until browned. Remove the sausage and drain the grease. Add 4 tablespoons of butter to the skillet and whisk in the flour. Gradually whisk in the milk and cook until the gravy thickens, 5 to 6 minutes.

2. Stir in the shredded cheddar and pepper jack cheeses, then season with the salt, pepper, garlic powder, and onion powder. Add the cooked sausage back into the gravy mixture.

Step 6: Assemble Casserole and Sandwiches

- Assemble casserole: Arrange the biscuits on top of the gravy mixture.

- Assemble, wrap, and label sandwiches: Once the eggs are finished baking, allow them to cool and then unmold them. Begin assembling the sandwiches: bottom bun, meat (sausage, bacon, or ham), cheese, egg, top bun. Wrap each sandwich in parchment paper and then foil, labeling each sandwich with the type and date.

Step 7: Bake Casserole

Cover the casserole and bake for 30 minutes. After 30 minutes, uncover and bake for an additional 15 to 20 minutes, until the biscuits are cooked through and golden brown.

Step 8: Cool and Store

Allow the casserole to cool slightly before portioning into meal prep containers.

STORAGE AND REHEATING

Freezer Breakfast Sandwiches:

- Store wrapped sandwiches in the freezer for up to 3 months.

- Thaw first, then remove the foil. Reheat in the microwave for 1 to 2 minutes or in the air fryer at 350°F for 5 minutes.

Biscuits and Gravy Casserole:

- Store in the fridge for up to 4 days. If storing for longer, freeze individual portions for up to a month.

- Reheat in the microwave for 2 to 3 minutes or in the oven at 350°F for 10 to 15 minutes.

BREAKFAST AND LUNCH
WEEKLY MEAL PREP PLAN

122

Bacon and Gruyère Egg Bites

127

Freezer Breakfast Sandwiches

293

Italian Grinder Pasta Salad

142

Cabbage Roll in a Bowl

Total servings: 27

- 5 servings of Bacon and Gruyère Egg Bites (2 egg bites per serving)
- 12 Freezer Breakfast Sandwiches
- 6 servings of Italian Grinder Pasta Salad
- 4 servings of Cabbage Roll in a Bowl

Total active time (prep work, assembly, cleanup): 1 hour 15 minutes

Total hands-off time: 1 hour 25 minutes (All recipes are either cooking or baking during this time, freeing you up for cleanup.)

Total meal prep time: 2 hours 40 minutes

TIME-SAVING SHORTCUTS

- *Buy precooked bacon.*
- *Buy bagged lettuce.*
- *Buy shredded cheese.*
- *Buy precooked rice.*

SHOPPING LIST

Don't forget to check your fridge, freezer, and pantry to take inventory of what you already have on hand and cross-reference it with the grocery list.

PRODUCE

- Cherry tomatoes
- Fresh flat-leaf parsley
- Garlic
- Green cabbage, 1 medium head
- Red onion, 1
- Romaine lettuce, 1 small head
- Sweet onion, 1

DAIRY AND EGGS

- American cheese, 4 slices
- Butter, 5 tablespoons
- Cottage cheese, 1 (16-ounce) container
- Crumbled feta cheese, 1 small container
- Eggs, 18
- Gruyère cheese, 1 small block
- Parmesan cheese, 1 small block
- Provolone cheese, 1 small block
- Swiss cheese, 1 small block
- White cheddar cheese, 1 small block

MEAT

- Bacon, 1 pound
- Canadian bacon, 8 slices
- Cooked sausage patties (English muffin size), 4
- Ground beef, 1½ pounds
- Ground pork, 8 ounces
- Hard salami
- Sliced ham

PANTRY

- Balsamic vinegar
- Beef stock, ¾ cup
- Black olives
- Canned artichoke hearts
- Canned chickpeas
- Cornstarch
- Diced tomatoes, 2 (15-ounce) cans
- Dijon mustard
- Dried oregano
- Dried thyme
- English muffins, 12
- Everything bagel seasoning (or make Herby Everything Seasoning, page 314)
- Garlic powder
- Hot sauce
- Italian seasoning
- Long-grain rice
- Mayonnaise, 1 cup
- Olive oil
- Onion powder
- Paprika
- Pepperoncini
- Red wine vinegar
- Tapioca starch
- Tomato paste, 1 (6-ounce) can
- Tri-color orecchiette pasta, 14 ounces
- White vinegar

GAME PLAN

Step 1: Gather Ingredients and Equipment

Bacon and Gruyère Egg Bites: blender, silicone egg bite molds with lid, Dutch oven (or large high-sided skillet with lid)

Freezer Breakfast Sandwiches: silicone muffin top pan, parchment paper, foil

Italian Grinder Pasta Salad: large mixing bowl, measuring spoons, large spoon for tossing

Cabbage Roll in a Bowl: large skillet or Dutch oven, spoon for stirring

Step 2: Prep Ingredients

Bacon and Gruyère Egg Bites:

1. Chop the cooked bacon and portion out the cheeses.

2. Blend the egg mixture and set it aside.

Freezer Breakfast Sandwiches:

1. Toast the English muffins. To save time, you can toast them all at once on a sheet pan in the oven.

2. Warm the sausage patties, bacon, and ham (even if using precooked) and set aside.

Italian Grinder Pasta Salad:

1. Cook the pasta as directed on the package and drain.

2. Chop the tomatoes, onions, pepperoncini, olives, and artichokes.

Cabbage Roll in a Bowl:

1. Dice the onion, mince the garlic, and slice the cabbage.

2. Cook the rice (if not already cooked).

Step 3: Assemble and Start Cooking

Bacon and Gruyère Egg Bites:

1. Blend the egg mixture as directed.

2. Add the bacon to the wells of the egg bite mold. Top with the cheese.

3. Fill with the egg mixture.

Freezer Breakfast Sandwiches:

1. Prepare the egg mixture in the blender and divide it between the wells of the muffin top pan.

2. Bake the eggs as directed.

Italian Grinder Pasta Salad:

1. Toss all of the chopped ingredients together in a large bowl.

2. Whisk the dressing ingredients and toss with the salad.

Cabbage Roll in a Bowl:

1. Cook the onions, garlic, ground beef, and pork.

2. Add the spices, stock, and tomatoes, then simmer for 5 minutes.

3. Add the cabbage and rice.

Step 4: Assemble and Finish Cooking

Bacon and Gruyère Egg Bites: Steam the egg bites per the recipe instructions for 12 to 15 minutes.

Freezer Breakfast Sandwiches: While the egg bites are cooking, assemble the sandwiches: bottom bun, meat, cheese, egg, top bun.

Italian Grinder Pasta Salad: Refrigerate the pasta salad while preparing the other dishes.

Cabbage Roll in a Bowl: Cook for 20 minutes, then simmer and reduce the heat.

Step 5: Cool and Store

Bacon and Gruyère Egg Bites: After cooling, remove the egg bites from the mold and allow to cool. Portion into meal prep containers, 2 egg bites per serving.

Freezer Breakfast Sandwiches: Wrap each sandwich in parchment and foil and label them accordingly. Put half of the sandwiches in the freezer and half in the refrigerator.

Italian Grinder Pasta Salad: Once chilled, portion into meal prep containers.

Cabbage Roll in a Bowl: After cooling, portion into meal prep containers. Garnish with fresh parsley before serving.

STORAGE AND REHEATING

Bacon and Gruyère Egg Bites:

- Store in the fridge for up to 5 days. Freeze any leftovers.

- Reheat in the microwave for 1 to 2 minutes or in the air fryer at 350°F for 5 minutes.

Freezer Breakfast Sandwiches:

- Store wrapped sandwiches in the freezer for up to 3 months.

- Thaw first, then remove the foil. Reheat in the microwave for 1 to 2 minutes or in the air fryer at 350°F for 5 minutes.

BREAKFAST AND LUNCH
WEEKLY MEAL PREP PLAN

OPTION **2**

281

French Toast Casserole

124

Baked Ham and Egg Skillet

216

Hoisin Beef Bowls

208

Chimichurri Chicken Salad Bowls

Total servings: 16

- 6 servings of French Toast Casserole
- 4 servings of Baked Ham and Egg Skillet
- 4 Hoisin Beef Bowls
- 2 Chimichurri Chicken Salad Bowls

Total active time (prep work, assembly, cleanup): 1 hour 30 minutes

Total hands-off time: 2 hours 20 minutes (All recipes are either cooking or baking during this time, freeing you up for cleanup.)

Total meal prep time: 3 hours 50 minutes

TIME-SAVING SHORTCUTS

- *Buy precooked rice for the beef bowls.*

- *Buy chopped veggies or bagged salad mix and/or rotisserie chicken for the chicken salad bowls.*

SHOPPING LIST

Don't forget to check your fridge, freezer, and pantry to take inventory of what you already have on hand and cross-reference it with the grocery list.

PRODUCE

- Avocado, 1 large
- Baby gem or butter lettuce, 2 heads
- Bell pepper, red, 1
- Carrot, 1
- Fresh basil
- Garlic
- Ginger root
- Grape tomatoes, 1 pint
- Green onions, 1 bunch
- Leek, 1
- Purple cabbage, ½ small head
- Strawberries

DAIRY AND EGGS

- Butter, 6 tablespoons
- Crumbled goat cheese, 1 small container
- Eggs, 14
- Gruyère cheese, 1 small block
- Heavy cream, ½ cup
- Milk, 1¾ cups
- Sour cream, ¼ cup

MEAT

- Cooked chicken (or rotisserie chicken), 10 ounces
- Cooked ham steak
- Ground beef, 2 pounds

PANTRY

- Balsamic vinegar
- Brioche buns, 8
- Brown sugar
- Canned artichoke hearts
- Canned chickpeas
- Cashews
- Chimichurri sauce
- Cinnamon
- Hoisin sauce, 6 tablespoons
- Maple syrup

- Nutmeg
- Pecans
- Pepperoncini
- Pesto
- Pickled red onion
- Rice
- Sesame seeds
- Soy sauce, 3 tablespoons
- Sriracha or chili paste
- Sunflower seeds
- Toasted sesame oil
- Tomato paste
- Vanilla bean paste

GAME PLAN

Step 1: Gather Ingredients and Equipment

French Toast Casserole: 9- by 13-inch baking dish, whisk, large mixing bowl, foil, small bowl

Baked Ham and Egg Skillet: ovenproof skillet, ramekins, whisk, wooden spoon

Hoisin Beef Bowls: large skillet, wooden spoon

Chimichurri Chicken Salad Bowls: large mixing bowl, small bowl

Step 2: Prepare Ingredients

French Toast Casserole:

1. Whisk together the eggs, milk, brown sugar, vanilla bean paste, cinnamon, salt, and nutmeg in a large mixing bowl.

2. Cut the brioche buns into 1-inch cubes.

3. Melt the butter for the topping and mix with the brown sugar and pecans.

Baked Ham and Egg Skillet:

1. Cube the ham and slice the leeks.

2. Whisk the heavy cream, sour cream, pesto, and salt.

3. Preheat the oven to 400°F.

Hoisin Beef Bowls:

1. Slice the bell pepper and julienne the carrot.

2. Shred or slice the cabbage.

3. Slice the green onions, separating the white and green parts.

4. Cook the rice (if not already cooked).

Chimichurri Chicken Salad Bowls:

1. Cube or shred the chicken.

2. Slice the avocado, tomatoes, and artichoke hearts.

3. Slice the red onion and pepperoncini.

4. Chop the lettuce into bite-sized pieces.

Step 3: Assemble and Start Cooking

French Toast Casserole:

1. Add the cubed bread to the egg mixture and toss until evenly coated. Let soak for 1 hour.

2. Pour the mixture into the greased 9- by 13-inch baking dish.

3. Drizzle the melted butter and sugar mixture over the top, then sprinkle with pecans.

Baked Ham and Egg Skillet:

1. Cook the ham and leeks in the butter until the leeks are soft and ham is crispy.

2. Whisk the cream mixture, pour into the skillet, and bring to a slow boil.

3. Add the cheese and ham-leek mixture, then crack the eggs into the sauce.

Hoisin Beef Bowls:

1. Prepare the rice and divide evenly among 4 storage containers.

2. Arrange the vegetables in sections on top of the rice.

3. In a small bowl, combine the hoisin sauce, soy sauce, tomato paste, brown sugar, and sriracha.

Chimichurri Chicken Salad Bowls:

1. Whisk together the chimichurri and balsamic vinegar for the dressing.

2. Assemble the salad: Divide the lettuce, chicken, avocado, tomatoes, chickpeas, artichokes, goat cheese, pepperoncini, and red onions into bowls. If you store all of the ingredients in separate containers (salad bar style), they will last longer in the fridge.

Step 4: Assemble and Finish Cooking

Baked Ham and Egg Skillet: Bake at 400°F for 12 to 15 minutes, until the eggs are set to your liking.

French Toast Casserole:

1. Let the casserole sit covered at room temperature while you bake the ham and egg skillet.

2. Reduce the oven temperature to 350°F and bake for 30 minutes, covered. Uncover and bake for an additional 15 minutes, until the topping is golden and the egg mixture is set.

Hoisin Beef Bowls:

1. While the casserole is baking, prepare the beef. Heat the sesame oil in a skillet, add the ground beef, and cook until browned.

2. Add the garlic, ginger, and white parts of the green onions.

3. Spoon the beef mixture over the assembled rice bowls and garnish.

Chimichurri Chicken Salad Bowls: No cooking involved—just refrigerate the salad until ready to serve.

Step 5: Cool and Store

French Toast Casserole and Baked Ham and Egg Skillet: After cooling, portion each recipe into meal prep containers. (The Hoisin Beef Bowls have already been portioned into containers.)

Chimichurri Chicken Salad Bowls: Portion into meal prep containers, storing the dressing separately to keep the salad fresh.

STORAGE AND REHEATING

French Toast Casserole:

- Store in the fridge for up to 4 days.

- Reheat in the microwave for 2 minutes or in the oven at 350°F for 10 minutes.

Baked Ham and Egg Skillet:

- Store in the fridge for up to 4 days.

- Reheat in the microwave for 1 to 2 minutes or in the oven at 350°F for 10 minutes.

Hoisin Beef Bowls:

- Store in the fridge for up to 4 days.

- Reheat in the microwave for 2 minutes or in a skillet over medium heat until warmed through.

Chimichurri Chicken Salad Bowls:

- Store in the fridge for up to 3 days. Drizzle with dressing and top with sunflower seeds when serving.

- Best served cold.

DINNER-ONLY
WEEKLY MEAL PREP PLAN

146

French Onion Chicken

211

California Roll in a Bowl

75

Gnocchi with Pancetta and Vegetables

Total servings: 10

- 4 servings of French Onion Chicken
- 2 servings of California Roll in a Bowl
- 4 servings of Gnocchi with Pancetta and Vegetables

Total active time (prep work, assembly, cleanup): 1 hour 15 minutes

Total hands-off time: 1 hour 15 minutes

Total meal prep time: 2 hours 30 minutes

TIME-SAVING SHORTCUTS

- *Buy precooked rice.*

SHOPPING LIST

Don't forget to check your fridge, freezer, and pantry to take inventory of what you already have on hand and cross-reference it with the grocery list.

PRODUCE

- Avocado, 1 medium
- Broccoli, 1 small head
- Cucumber (English or Persian), 1
- Fresh rosemary
- Fresh sage
- Fresh thyme
- Garlic, 1 head
- Grape tomatoes, 1 pint
- Red onion, 1 medium
- Shredded carrots, ½ cup
- Sweet potato, 1 large
- Yellow onions, 2 medium

DAIRY

- Butter, 4 tablespoons
- Gruyère cheese, 1 small block
- Parmesan cheese, 1 small block
- Potato gnocchi, 1 (20-ounce) package
- Shredded mozzarella cheese, 1 cup

MEAT

- Boneless, skinless chicken breasts, 4 (6 ounces each)
- Imitation crab meat (surimi), 8 ounces
- Pancetta, 8 ounces

PANTRY

- Balsamic vinegar
- Beef stock, 1 cup
- Black sesame seeds
- Cooking sherry, ½ cup
- Dried seaweed snack sheets, 4 (or 1 nori sheet)
- Olive oil
- Pickled ginger
- Red pepper flakes
- Soy sauce
- Sugar
- Sushi rice
- Unseasoned rice vinegar
- Wasabi paste
- Worcestershire sauce
- Yum yum sauce (or make your own, page 306)

GAME PLAN

Step 1: Gather Ingredients and Equipment

French Onion Chicken: large ovenproof skillet, tongs

California Roll in a Bowl: mixing bowl, small bowl

Gnocchi with Pancetta and Vegetables: sheet pan, parchment paper, mixing bowl

Step 2: Prepare Ingredients

French Onion Chicken:

1. Season the chicken breasts with salt and pepper on both sides.

2. Thinly slice the onions and mince the garlic.

California Roll in a Bowl:

1. Prepare the sushi rice.

2. Slice the avocado, cucumber, and carrots. Cut the imitation crab into bite-sized pieces.

Gnocchi with Pancetta and Vegetables:

1. Cube the sweet potato.

2. Cut the broccoli into florets.

3. Slice the onion.

4. Mince the garlic.

Step 3: Assemble and Start Cooking

French Onion Chicken:

1. In a large skillet, melt 2 tablespoons of butter. Cook the onions and garlic over medium-low heat until caramelized, about 30 minutes. Set aside.

2. In the same skillet, add the remaining butter, then pan-sear the chicken on both sides. Remove from the pan and set aside.

California Roll in a Bowl:

1. Whisk together the rice vinegar, sugar, and salt. Toss with the cooked sushi rice.

2. Divide the rice between bowls and top with the imitation crab, avocado, seaweed, cucumber, and carrots. Drizzle with yum yum sauce and sprinkle with sesame seeds.

Gnocchi with Pancetta and Vegetables:

1. Preheat the oven to 450°F and line a sheet pan with parchment paper.

2. Toss the gnocchi, pancetta, sweet potato, broccoli, tomatoes, and red onion in olive oil, balsamic vinegar, garlic, Parmesan, sage, rosemary, salt, pepper, and red pepper flakes.

3. Spread the mixture on the sheet pan in a single layer.

Step 4: Assemble and Finish Cooking

French Onion Chicken:

1. Deglaze the pan with the beef stock, scraping up the browned bits.

2. Add the sherry, garlic, Worcestershire, thyme, salt, and pepper. Simmer for 6 minutes, then return the onions and chicken to the pan.

3. Bake at 275°F for 7 to 8 minutes, until the cheese is melted. Garnish with fresh thyme.

California Roll in a Bowl: Drizzle yum yum sauce over the assembled bowls. Serve with soy sauce, pickled ginger, and wasabi in a container on the side.

Gnocchi with Pancetta and Vegetables: Bake at 450°F for 20 minutes, or until tender. Drizzle with olive oil and serve with extra Parmesan.

Step 5: Cool and Store

After cooling, portion each recipe into meal prep containers.

STORAGE AND REHEATING

French Onion Chicken:

- Store in the fridge for up to 4 days.

- Reheat in the microwave for 2 minutes or in a skillet over low heat until warmed through.

California Roll in a Bowl:

- Store in the fridge for up to 3 days.

- Best served cold.

Gnocchi with Pancetta and Vegetables:

- Store in the fridge for up to 4 days.

- Reheat in the microwave for 2 minutes or on the stovetop with a drizzle of olive oil over medium heat until warmed through.

DINNER-ONLY
WEEKLY MEAL PREP PLAN

68

Roasted Salmon and
Vegetables

137

Jambalaya

103

Copycat Hamburger
Helper Beef Stroganoff

Total servings: 12

- 4 servings of Roasted Salmon and Vegetables
- 4 servings of Jambalaya
- 4 servings of Copycat Hamburger Helper Beef Stroganoff

Total active time (prep work, assembly, cleanup): 1 hour 25 minutes

Total hands-off time: 1 hour 10 minutes (All recipes are either cooking or baking during this time, freeing you up for cleanup.)

Total meal prep time: 2 hours 35 minutes

TIME-SAVING SHORTCUTS

- *Buy precooked rice.*
- *Buy chopped vegetables.*

SHOPPING LIST

Don't forget to check your fridge, freezer, and pantry to take inventory of what you already have on hand and cross-reference it with the grocery list.

PRODUCE

- Bell pepper, green, 1
- Bell pepper, red, 1
- Bell pepper, yellow, 1
- Broccoli, 1 small head
- Celery, 3 ribs
- Fresh dill
- Fresh flat-leaf parsley
- Garlic, 1 head
- Green onions, 1 bunch
- Lemon, 1
- Red onions, 2 small
- Shiitake mushrooms, 6 ounces
- Yellow onions, 1 medium, 1 small
- Zucchini, 1 large

DAIRY

- Butter, 3 tablespoons
- Sour cream, 12 ounces

MEAT

- Andouille sausage, 1 pound
- Boneless, skinless chicken thighs, 1½ pounds
- Ground beef, 1 pound
- Raw shrimp, 1 pound
- Salmon fillets, 4 (6 ounces each)

PANTRY

- All-purpose flour
- Beef stock, 1 cup
- Cajun seasoning
- Capers
- Casarecce pasta, 12 ounces
- Cayenne pepper (optional)
- Chicken stock, 2½ cups
- Diced tomatoes, 1 (14.5-ounce) can
- Dijon mustard
- Dried basil
- Garlic powder
- Long-grain white rice, 1¼ cups
- Olive oil, ½ cup
- Onion powder
- Smoked paprika
- Worcestershire sauce

GAME PLAN

Step 1: Gather Ingredients and Equipment

Roasted Salmon and Vegetables: sheet pan, parchment paper, small bowl

Jambalaya: large skillet or Dutch oven, mixing spoon

Copycat Hamburger Helper Beef Stroganoff: large pot, large skillet, mixing spoon

Step 2: Prepare Ingredients

Roasted Salmon and Vegetables:

1. Preheat the oven to 425°F. Line a sheet pan with parchment paper.

2. Season the salmon fillets with salt and pepper.

Jambalaya:

1. Slice the sausage into ¼-inch-thick slices.

2. Cut the chicken thighs into bite-sized pieces.

3. Chop the celery, bell peppers, and onions. Slice the green onions, separating the green and white parts. Mince the garlic.

Copycat Hamburger Helper Beef Stroganoff:

1. Dice the onion and mince the garlic.

2. Slice the mushrooms.

3. Cook the pasta according to the package instructions.

Step 3: Assemble and Cook

Roasted Salmon and Vegetables:

1. In a small bowl, combine the olive oil, capers, mustard, dill, salt, pepper, and garlic.

2. Brush the salmon fillets with the marinade. Arrange the vegetables around the salmon on the sheet pan. Toss the vegetables in half of the remaining marinade.

3. Roast for 20 minutes, or until the salmon is cooked through and vegetables are crisp-tender.

Jambalaya:

1. Heat the olive oil in a large skillet over medium-high heat. Sear the sausage and chicken until browned. Remove and set aside.

2. In the same pan, combine the butter and flour. Stir to form a roux.

3. Add the onion, garlic, celery, and bell peppers and cook for 3 minutes. Add the tomatoes, spices, and stock and bring to a simmer.

4. Return the rice, chicken, and sausage to the skillet. Cover and cook for 15 minutes. Add the shrimp and cook for 5 more minutes.

Copycat Hamburger Helper Beef Stroganoff:

1. Heat the olive oil in a large skillet. Add the onions and cook until translucent. Add the garlic and cook for 2 minutes.

2. Brown the ground beef in the same skillet. Drain the excess grease.

3. Stir in the Worcestershire sauce, mushrooms, and spices. Cook for 6 minutes.

4. Add the stock and sour cream. Bring to a boil, then reduce to a simmer. Add the cooked pasta and stir to combine.

Step 4: Assemble and Garnish

Roasted Salmon and Vegetables: Drizzle the remaining marinade over the salmon and vegetables. Garnish with fresh dill, a squeeze of lemon, and cracked black pepper.

Jambalaya: Garnish with sliced green onions and serve.

Copycat Hamburger Helper Beef Stroganoff: Toss the cooked pasta into the beef mixture. Garnish with parsley before serving.

Step 5: Cool and Store

After cooling, portion each recipe into meal prep containers.

STORAGE AND REHEATING

Roasted Salmon and Vegetables:

- Store in the fridge for up to 4 days.

- Reheat in the microwave for 2 to 3 minutes or in the oven at 350°F until warmed through.

Jambalaya:

- Store in the fridge for up to 4 days.

- Reheat in the microwave for 2 minutes or on the stovetop with a splash of water or stock over medium heat until warmed through.

Copycat Hamburger Helper Beef Stroganoff:

- Store in the fridge for up to 4 days.

- Reheat in the microwave for 2 minutes or on the stovetop over medium heat until warmed through.

10 TIPS FOR BUDGET GROCERY SHOPPING

Grocery shopping is where every great meal begins. While it's easy to go overboard when shopping, it doesn't have to break the bank. With the right strategies, you can save money, reduce food waste, and still prioritize quality and flavor. Here are ten essential tips for budget-friendly shopping.

1 **SET A BUDGET AND STICK TO IT** Calculate your monthly food allowance: Start with your total take-home income and subtract essential expenses (rent, utilities, car payments, insurance, savings, etc.). Allocate a realistic amount for groceries. Be honest with your priorities—food is essential, but dining out and treats can be budgeted separately if there is money left over.

Set a budget and stick to it: Now that you know how much you can spend monthly, divide those funds into weekly budgets. Some weeks you may spend less and some weeks you may need to spend more. Just make sure that your total spending for the month is equal to or less than the dollar amount you've allocated to groceries.

Take inventory before shopping: Check your pantry, fridge, and freezer to see what you already have before heading to the store. Cross-reference this with your grocery list to avoid buying duplicates. When possible, plan your weekly meals around the food items you have on hand.

Pay for groceries in cash: Paying in cash can help you stick to a strict food budget. Avoid paying with a credit card whenever possible, unless you can pay it off each month. The interest you would incur would significantly increase what you are actually spending on groceries in the long run, thus blowing your budget.

Utilize loyalty and rewards programs: Sign up for store reward programs and apps for access to exclusive discounts and coupons. This will help stretch your budget further.

Take advantage of midweek sales: Many stores roll out new sales midweek. Check your store's flyers or apps for weekly specials. Write your meal plan according to what's on sale. (See "Mastering Meal Prep," page 8.)

> *Pro Tip: Watch the unit price. Compare prices by looking at the cost per ounce or per pound to get the best value, even if it means switching brands or opting for a larger size.*

2  **SHOP WITH A LIST AND A GAME PLAN**

Grocery shopping without a list and a game plan is like wandering the wilderness without a compass and a map. A clear, intentional shopping list keeps you focused, prevents overspending, and reduces food waste. Here's how to make your list work for you:

Plan your meals: Identify recipes you want to cook for the week and cross-reference the ingredient lists with the ingredients you already have in your fridge, freezer, and pantry.

Shop on a full stomach: Hunger can turn your shopping cart into a mountain of expensive impulse buys. Eat a snack before shopping to stay focused and on budget.

Stick to the list (except when...): Make a list, but stay open to substitutions if something unexpected is discounted. Be flexible regarding sales, but don't get sidetracked by nonessentials.

Organize by section: Divide your list into categories (produce, dairy, meats, pantry staples, frozen foods) and arrange them in an order that makes sense for the layout of your usual grocery store. Doing so helps you shop efficiently and avoid backtracking through aisles. It will also help ensure that you don't forget anything.

Shop the perimeter: The store's outer edges usually house fresh produce, dairy, and proteins, while the aisles are packed with processed options. Stick to the perimeter for healthier and often more cost-effective choices.

> *Pro Tip:* Keep a magnetic notepad or whiteboard on your fridge, or a note in your phone, and jot down items as you run out. Transfer these to your shopping list before heading to the store.

3  **SHOP SEASONALLY**

Seasonal produce is a game-changer: It's fresher, more flavorful, and often more affordable. Here's how to make the most of seasonal shopping:

Know your seasons: Learn when fruits and vegetables are at their peak and plan your meals accordingly. Strawberries in summer, squash in fall—shopping seasonally is not only budget-friendly but also ensures better quality and taste. Fresh tomatoes in summer? Think caprese salads and marinara sauces. Squash in fall? It's soup and roasted veggie season.

Freeze or preserve: Stock up on seasonal produce when prices are low. Then you can freeze, can, or pickle extras for later.

Try a CSA: Community supported agriculture (CSA) programs deliver fresh, seasonal, local produce straight to you (or allow you to pick up at a nearby location). It's a win for farmers, the environment, and your wallet.

Pro Tip: To maximize your seasonal produce, consider creating a "seasonal staples" list for each season. This way, you can consistently incorporate the best ingredients into your meals, ensuring variety and flavor year-round while taking advantage of peak produce.

4 SAVE MONEY ON MEAT, SEAFOOD, FRUIT, AND VEGETABLES

Buy cheaper cuts of meat: Instead of chicken breasts, buy chicken thighs. Not only are they cheaper, but they are also more flavorful. Instead of cuts like filet mignon, rib eye, or New York strip, opt for less-expensive but still tender cuts like top sirloin, chuck eye, tri-tip, or flat-iron steak.

Buy whole: A whole chicken or fish is always more economical than individual cuts, and you can use the leftovers for stock or additional meals. Take it a step further and go in with a group of friends or family on a whole cow.

Consider meat and seafood subscriptions: Meat and seafood subscription delivery services can provide high-quality proteins at discounted prices. Many services allow customization, ensuring you get only the ingredients you need and will use. Look for options that support local farmers.

Explore meat alternatives: Lentils, chickpeas, tofu, tempeh, and eggs are protein-rich and budget-friendly meat alternatives.

Buy whole fruits and vegetables: Don't be tempted by prepped produce. For example, a whole butternut squash tends to cost half as much as the cut-up pieces that come in a plastic container. Plus, if you purchase a whole squash, you also get seeds for roasting and scraps for stock. Same goes for fruit like pineapple. Have you ever checked the price difference between a whole pineapple and a small container of precut pineapple? Precut produce also spoils faster, so buying whole helps reduce food waste.

Don't be afraid of frozen or canned produce: They are fantastic options. They're picked at peak ripeness, often just as nutritious as fresh, and far more affordable. They are an especially good option if you are someone who frequently finds yourself with a fridge full of spoiled produce.

Shop farmers' markets: Local markets often have the freshest produce at competitive prices. Go late in the day for potential discounts as vendors clear their stock. Depending on the size and location of the market, you can usually get great deals from meat and seafood vendors as well.

Take advantage of CSA benefits: Again, community supported agriculture boxes deliver seasonal, local produce right to your door, often at a lower cost than grocery stores.

> *Pro Tip:* Roast a whole chicken each week as part of your meal prep, and then use the meat in multiple meals. But don't let anything go to waste—simmer the bones with leftover vegetable scraps, garlic, seasoning, and water to make a homemade stock.

5 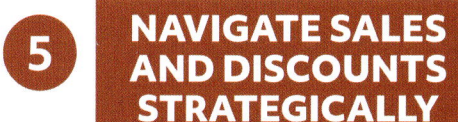 NAVIGATE SALES AND DISCOUNTS STRATEGICALLY

Shop with intention: Just because something is on sale doesn't mean you need it. Ask yourself, "Would I buy this at full price?"

Use coupons and apps: Many grocery stores offer digital coupons or loyalty apps that give you access to exclusive discounts. Most stores even allow you to stack these with manufacturer coupons.

Look for clearance racks: Check for markdowns on items nearing their sell-by dates. Meat, dairy, and baked goods are often discounted and can be used immediately or frozen for later.

> *Pro Tip:* Pick the "ugly" produce. Many stores offer slightly blemished fruits and veggies at a discount. They taste just as great in soups, stews, or smoothies.

Understand unit pricing: Check those little shelf tags to compare costs per ounce or pound. It's the easiest way to see if the family-sized box is truly the better deal.

6 GENERIC VERSUS NAME BRANDS: KNOW WHEN IT MATTERS

Don't underestimate store-brand products. They're often just as good as the name brands at a fraction of the price. In many cases, they are  even made by the same companies and produced in the same manufacturing plants. Here's where to save and where to splurge:

Save on basics: Store-brand pantry staples like canned goods, pasta, flour, and sugar are reliable and cost-effective.

Splurge on specialty items: For ingredients where flavor and quality matter more, like cheeses, olive oil, and coffee, invest in trusted brands.

When in doubt, try it out: Experiment with generic products and find ones you love. More often than not, you may find yourself pleasantly surprised, and you'll have a little extra room in your grocery budget for a small treat.

> **Pro Tip:** *Look for guarantees. Many stores stand behind their private-label products with satisfaction guarantees, so if you're not happy, you can often return the product for a full refund.*

7 · EMBRACE BULK SHOPPING

Buying in bulk can save you money in the long run, as long as you shop wisely and avoid buying more than you can reasonably use before it spoils.

Stock up on pantry staples: Dry goods such as rice, beans, pasta, oats, nuts, and flours are considerably cheaper when purchased in bulk.

Avoid perishable pitfalls: Only buy perishable items in bulk if you're confident you'll use them before they spoil. Consider portioning out and freezing bread, meat, vegetables, or even dairy products if you buy them in larger quantities.

Split large quantities: Share the cost of larger quantities with friends or family to save money and avoid waste.

> **Pro Tip:** *Bring reusable containers to stores with bulk bins to reduce waste and measure exactly what you need. Use clear containers to store bulk purchases. It helps you see what you have and avoid overbuying.*

8 · BUILD A WELL-STOCKED PANTRY

A stocked pantry is the backbone of affordable and flexible cooking. Focus on building a pantry filled with versatile staples that have a long shelf life. These are good items to stock up on when they are on sale.

Dry goods: Rice, quinoa, pasta, beans, lentils, nuts and seeds, oats, flour, sugar, coffee. You can typically save a lot of money by buying these items in bulk.

Canned and jarred goods: Tomatoes, peppers, olives, beans, fruits, vegetables, tuna and salmon, sauces, dressings, stocks, soups. These are also great items to consider purchasing generic versus name brand.

Condiments: Soy sauce, coconut aminos, hot sauce, honey, syrups, chili crisp, nut butters. These are all excellent flavor enhancers.

Herbs and spices: Garlic powder, onion powder, dried minced onion, Italian seasoning, paprika, chili powder, cumin, oregano, ground ginger, and bay leaves. A well-stocked spice rack can transform the simplest of ingredients. Start small with these ten and build your collection over time.

Oils and vinegars: Olive oil, avocado oil, coconut oil, toasted sesame oil, balsamic vinegar, unseasoned rice vinegar, apple cider vinegar, red wine vinegar, white vinegar. These types cover most bases.

> **Pro Tip:** *Build your pantry gradually. Add one or two staple items each trip instead of overloading your budget by buying them all at once.*

9 **REDUCE FOOD WASTE AND STRETCH YOUR INGREDIENTS**

Stretching your groceries not only saves money but also reduces waste. Here are some ways to make every ingredient count:

Use every part of the ingredient: Save vegetable scraps for homemade stock, use bones for broth, or repurpose stale bread into croutons or breadcrumbs.

Store food properly: Learn the best ways to store produce, dairy, meat, and seafood in both the fridge and freezer to extend their shelf life.

Repurpose leftovers: For example, roast veggies one day, and then toss them into soups, pastas, or frittatas the next. (For lots of great ideas, flip to the Repurposing Leftovers chapter.)

Know what keeps: Hardy vegetables like carrots, cabbage, and potatoes will last for weeks when stored properly. Prioritize these over delicate greens that are prone to quick spoilage if you're shopping for longer periods.

> **Pro Tip:** *Designate a "Use Me First" bin in your fridge for ingredients nearing expiration. Prioritize meals that will utilize these ingredients.*

10 SHOP ONLINE FOR CONVENIENCE AND CONTROL

Online grocery shopping has become a powerful tool for budget-conscious shoppers. Not only is it convenient, but it can save you a lot of money through exclusive online savings and reducing impulse purchases you might make in person. Here are some tips:

Save your favorites: Most platforms let you save a list of frequently purchased items, making it easy to reorder essentials and cut down on browsing time.

Avoid impulse buys: Shopping online eliminates the temptation of browsing aisles without intention and adding items to your cart that are not on your grocery list.

Track your spending: Most online platforms show you a running total as you shop, making it easier to stay within budget.

Compare prices: Easily compare prices between brands and stores within one app or website. Many grocery stores and big box stores have apps and websites that also give you access to exclusive online coupons and discounts that are not available in store.

> ***Pro Tip:*** *Order online but schedule curbside pickup to save time and avoid delivery fees.*

SMART STORAGE

Produce:

Fruits: Store most fruits (like apples, pears, and citrus) in the fridge's crisper drawer. However, keep fruits like bananas, avocados, and tomatoes at room temperature until ripe.

Vegetables and Herbs: Leafy greens and herbs should be wrapped in a damp paper towel and placed in a sealed container in the fridge. Alternatively, store fresh herbs upright in a jar of water with about 1 inch of water. If buying precut lettuce, store it in a paper towel–lined container. Vegetables like potatoes, onions, squash, and garlic do best in a cool, dark pantry.

Dairy:

Store milk, cheese, and yogurt in the coldest part of the fridge, usually toward the back. Keep them in their original packaging and make sure to seal containers tightly to prevent spoilage.

For butter, keep it in the fridge for long-term storage, but you can leave a small amount at room temperature for easier spreading.

Meat & Seafood:

Meat: Store fresh meat on trays at the bottom of the fridge, and use within 2 to 3 days of purchase. If you're not going to use it right away, freeze it.

Seafood: Fresh seafood should be used within 1 to 2 days of purchase. Store it on a bed of ice in the fridge or freeze it if you plan to keep it longer.

SHEET
PAN
RECIPES

There are few cooking methods as simple, yet endlessly versatile, as the sheet pan meal. In a world of busy weeknights and endless to-do lists, sheet pan recipes are a saving grace for cooks of all skill levels. With a single baking sheet, a handful of ingredients, and a hot oven, you can quickly create a satisfying and balanced meal.

Preparing a sheet pan meal involves placing a variety of ingredients—protein, vegetables, and sometimes grains—on a large rimmed baking sheet, seasoning them, and roasting everything together in the oven. The goal is to have the entire meal cooked at once, so you should choose and arrange the ingredients with this in mind.

Sheet pan cooking isn't just about tossing food onto a tray and hoping for the best, though on some days, that carefree approach might do just fine. It's about layering flavors, mastering heat, and knowing how to work with your ingredients to maximize their taste and texture. Whether you're making a simpler recipe like Roasted Blackened Chicken and Vegetables (page 66) or a more decadent recipe like Crab and Shrimp–Stuffed Salmon with Caper-Dill Hollandaise (page 71) the sheet pan really does it all, with minimal hands-on time required.

CHOOSING the RIGHT PAN

Before we dive into technique, let's talk about the equipment. Not all sheet pans are created equal, and investing in the right one makes all the difference.

The sheet pan itself: A well-made sheet pan will last you years, if not decades. For durability and consistent cooking, look for a heavy-duty half sheet pan. The ideal sized pan measures about 18 by 13 inches and has a 1-inch lip to contain juices and prevent spills. Avoid thin, flimsy pans that will warp under high heat and lead to uneven cooking and frustration.

Materials matter: Aluminum sheet pans are the gold standard. They heat evenly and are lightweight and easy to clean. Stainless-steel pans work too, but they often don't conduct heat as efficiently. Nonstick pans are great for easy cleanup, but they're not ideal for high heat or broiling, as the coating can break down.

Liner or no liner: Knowing whether to line your sheet pan, and with what, can ensure better meals and make cleanup much easier.

- **No liner:** Ideal for foods that benefit from browning and crisping, like chicken, potatoes, and certain other vegetables.

- **Parchment:** Best for delicate foods like fish and shrimp, and for baking to prevent sticking and ensure easy removal.

- **Foil:** Useful for easy cleanup, particularly for sticky or saucy foods and foods that may release moisture, like pork chops and marinated proteins.

- **Racks and accessories:** For next-level sheet pan cooking, consider a wire rack that fits snugly inside your pan. This allows air to circulate under the food, leading to extra crispy textures.

MASTERING HEAT

Sheet pan cooking is about letting your oven do the heavy lifting, but understanding how to use heat effectively can turn good meals into great ones. Here are some general guidelines to follow.

High-heat roasting: Roasting at temperatures between 425°F and 450°F caramelizes the natural sugars in vegetables and proteins, creating crispy edges and deep flavor. This method is perfect for root vegetables, hearty greens (like broccoli and Brussels sprouts), and bone-in meats.

Moderate-heat roasting: Cooking at 375°F to 400°F works well for delicate proteins, like fish and shrimp, and vegetables that cook quickly, such as zucchini and bell peppers. It's also ideal when you want ingredients to cook evenly without too much browning.

Low-and-slow roasting: While less common for sheet pans, low-and-slow cooking at around 300°F is perfect for producing tender, juicy proteins like pork shoulder. This method gives you plenty of hands-off time while the flavors of the ingredients come together.

Broiling: When you need a blast of high heat to finish a dish or add crispy, golden edges, turn to the broiler. Broiling works wonders for cheese-topped dishes, glazed proteins, and finishing roasted vegetables.

TIMING

Cooking times may vary based on the size of the pieces of food, your oven's performance, and personal preferences. Keep these points in mind:

- **Preheat:** Preheat the oven before placing the sheet pan inside to achieve optimal results.

- **Watch carefully:** Cooking times can vary based on several factors—the density of the food being cooked, oven type, age of oven, elevation, etc.—so be sure to keep an eye on the food as it cooks.

- **Check for doneness:** Always use a meat thermometer to ensure proteins reach the appropriate internal temperatures for safety and desired doneness.

SAFE COOKING BY PROTEIN TYPE

Steak

- Rare: 120–130°F
- Medium rare: 130–135°F
- Medium: 135–145°F
- Medium well: 145–155°F
- Well done: 155°F+ (rest for 5 minutes)

Pork

- Medium rare: 145°F (rest for 3 minutes)
- Medium: 150°F
- Medium well: 155°F
- Well done: 160°F+

Chicken & Turkey

- Whole & pieces: 165°F (check thickest part)
- Ground Poultry: 165°F

Duck Breast

- Medium rare: 130–135°F
- Medium: 135–145°F
- Medium well: 150–160°F
- Well done: 165°F+

Lamb & Veal

- Rare: 125°F
- Medium rare: 130–135°F
- Medium: 135–145°F
- Medium well: 145–155°F
- Well done: 160°F+ (rest for 5 minutes)

Fish & Seafood

- Medium rare: 125–130°F
- Medium: 130–140°F
- Well done: 145°F+ (opaque and flakes easily)

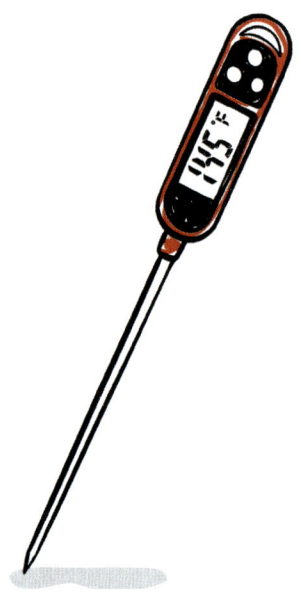

TIPS and TRICKS for SHEET PAN SUCCESS

With a little know-how and some practice, the sky is the limit when it comes to sheet pan meals. Here are some simple tips to ensure that your sheet pan recipes turn out perfect every time.

Cut evenly: Cut each ingredient into similar-size pieces based on their cooking time. Denser vegetables like carrots and potatoes should be smaller, while quick-cooking vegetables like zucchini and asparagus can be left larger.

Don't overcrowd the pan: Spread your ingredients in a single layer with space between pieces. Overcrowding traps steam and leads to soggy food instead of golden, crispy goodness.

Be mindful of timing: If necessary, start with the ingredients that take the longest to cook, like meats or root vegetables, and add quicker-cooking items later. For example, toss your broccoli onto the pan 10 minutes after your potatoes have started roasting.

Boost flavor: Sheet pan meals are a blank canvas for flavor. Use spice rubs, marinades, or infused oils to season your ingredients before cooking, and finish with fresh herbs, a squeeze of citrus, or a drizzle of sauce for brightness.

Double up for leftovers: Sheet pan recipes are perfect for meal prep. Roast twice the amount of protein or vegetables you need for today's meal, then use the leftovers in salads, protein bowls, pasta dishes, and casseroles later in the week.

Clean immediately: To make cleanup even easier, soak your sheet pan in warm water and dish soap as soon as it's cool. Stubborn spots? A little Bar Keepers Friend or a paste made with baking soda and water works like magic.

MUFFULETTA CHICKEN

¼ cup (½ stick) salted butter

4 (6-ounce) boneless, skinless chicken breasts (about 1½ pounds)

4 ounces salami, thinly sliced

4 ounces provolone cheese, sliced

4 ounces mortadella, thinly sliced

4 ounces mozzarella cheese, sliced

4 ounces capicola, thinly sliced

2 cups Olive Salad (page 308)

1. Preheat the oven to 350°F.

2. In a large skillet, melt the butter over medium to medium-high heat. Add the chicken breasts and sear until golden brown and caramelized, about 8 minutes on each side.

3. Transfer the chicken to a sheet pan. Top each breast with layers of salami, provolone, mortadella, mozzarella, and capicola. Bake for 10 minutes, until the cheese is melted and the deli meats are warmed through.

4. Top with a heaping portion of olive salad and serve.

TIPS & NOTES

- *Got leftovers? See page 339 for ideas for using them.*

- *Searing the chicken in butter not only locks in moisture but also creates a flavorful crust that adds depth to the dish. Don't rush this step— let the chicken develop a deep golden brown before flipping.*

- *Feel free to swap in smoked turkey or ham if you prefer a milder flavor. You can also use prosciutto or pepperoni.*

- *Provolone and mozzarella are classic, but Gouda, fontina, and Swiss are all excellent substitutions.*

HERBED BUTTER SPATCHCOCKED CHICKEN

SERVES: **4**

PREP TIME: **20 MINUTES**

COOK TIME: **70 MINUTES**

1 whole chicken (about 4 pounds)

6 tablespoons salted butter, softened

2 tablespoons chopped fresh thyme

1 tablespoon chopped fresh rosemary

2 teaspoons rubbed sage

2 teaspoons dried minced onion

1 teaspoon garlic powder

1 teaspoon sea salt

½ teaspoon black pepper

¼ cup chicken stock

1½ pounds red potatoes, quartered

12 ounces Brussels sprouts, halved

2 small red onions, cut into wedges

1. Preheat the oven to 425°F. Place a wire rack on top of a sheet pan.

2. To spatchcock the chicken: Place the chicken, breast side down, on a cutting board. Using kitchen shears, cut along one side of the spine, then the other, then remove the spine completely. Flip the chicken over, breast side up, and press down on the breastbone with the palm of your hand to flatten it. Pat the chicken dry with paper towels.

3. In a small bowl, mix together the butter, thyme, rosemary, sage, dried onion, garlic powder, salt, and pepper until well combined. Loosen the skin over the chicken breast with your fingers, creating a pocket. Pack half of the herb butter under the skin, then rub the remaining butter all over the top of the chicken.

4. Set the chicken breast side up on the rack. Pour the stock into the pan. Roast for 30 minutes.

5. Remove the pan from the oven. Remove the chicken and the rack. Add the potatoes, Brussels sprouts, and red onions to the pan, tossing them in the juices. Nestle the chicken in the pan, directly on top of the vegetables.

6. Return the pan to the oven and roast for another 35 to 50 minutes, until the chicken is crispy and golden brown and the thickest part of the breast is cooked to 165°F. If the Brussels sprouts are browning too quickly, pull them out early and pop them back in just before serving.

7. Let the chicken rest for at least 15 minutes before carving. For extra-crispy meat, shred the chicken and return it to the oven for 10 minutes. Serve straight from the pan for a rustic, easy-cleanup meal.

TIPS & NOTES

- *If spatchcocking the chicken yourself seems too intimidating, you can ask the butcher at the meat counter to do it for you.*

- *I like to serve this chicken with my Kale, Spinach, and Romaine Caesar (page 207) and a nice crusty bread to sop up the delicious pan juices.*

- *To make this dish dairy free, substitute ghee or butter-flavored coconut oil for the butter.*

- *Add smoked paprika to the herbed butter for a smoky kick.*

ROASTED BLACKENED CHICKEN and VEGETABLES

SERVES: **4**

PREP TIME: **20 MINUTES**

COOK TIME: **30 MINUTES**

4 (6-ounce) boneless, skinless chicken breasts (about 1½ pounds)

3 tablespoons Blackened Seasoning (page 315)

Juice of 1 large orange

1 tablespoon olive oil

1 tablespoon toasted sesame oil

1 teaspoon Dijon mustard

Sea salt and black pepper, to taste

1 small head broccoli, cut into florets

1 small red bell pepper, seeded and cut into large chunks

1 small yellow bell pepper, seeded and cut into large chunks

1 small green bell pepper, seeded and cut into large chunks

1 zucchini, cubed

2 small red onions, cut into wedges

½ cup halved green olives

Fresh orange slices, for serving

1. Preheat the oven to 425°F. Line a sheet pan with parchment paper.

2. Season the chicken breasts on both sides with the blackened seasoning and arrange in a single layer on the prepared pan.

3. For the dressing, whisk together the orange juice, olive oil, sesame oil, mustard, salt, and pepper. Combine the broccoli, peppers, zucchini, and onions in a mixing bowl. Pour half of the dressing over the vegetables and toss until they are evenly coated.

4. Arrange the vegetables around the chicken on the sheet pan and add the olives. Roast for 20 to 25 minutes, until the chicken is cooked through (165°F internal temperature) and the vegetables are tender.

5. Pour the remaining dressing over the chicken and vegetables and finish under the broiler on high for 3 to 5 minutes to add a little char and crispy edges to the vegetables. Serve with orange slices.

TIPS & NOTES

- *This dish is delicious served with Garlic-Herb Mashed Potatoes (page 189).*

- *I love to repurpose any leftovers into a big hearty salad tossed with Avocado Ranch Dressing (page 304) or wrap them in naan or a pita and top with Cucumber Sauce (page 307).*

ROASTED SALMON and VEGETABLES

SERVES: **4**

PREP TIME: **20 MINUTES**

COOK TIME: **20 MINUTES**

4 (6-ounce) skin-on salmon fillets

1½ teaspoons sea salt, divided

¾ teaspoon black pepper, divided

¼ cup olive oil

2 tablespoons drained capers

2 teaspoons Dijon mustard

2 teaspoons chopped fresh dill, plus extra for garnish

1 teaspoon garlic powder, or 2 cloves garlic, minced

1 small head broccoli, cut into florets

1 red bell pepper, seeded and cut into chunks

1 yellow bell pepper, seeded and cut into chunks

2 small red onions, cut into wedges

1 large zucchini, cut into chunks

1 lemon, cut into wedges, for serving

Cracked black pepper, for serving

1. Preheat the oven to 425°F. Line a sheet pan with parchment paper.

2. Season the salmon generously on all sides with 1 teaspoon of the salt and ½ teaspoon of the pepper.

3. For the dressing, whisk together the olive oil, capers, mustard, dill, garlic powder or minced garlic, remaining ½ teaspoon of salt, and remaining ¼ teaspoon of pepper in a small bowl.

4. Arrange the salmon on the prepared pan and brush with some of the dressing. Arrange the broccoli, peppers, onions, and zucchini around the salmon in a single layer. Toss the vegetables with half of the remaining dressing.

5. Roast the salmon and vegetables for 20 minutes, or until the salmon is cooked through and the vegetables start to get a slight char and are crisp-tender.

6. To serve, drizzle the remaining dressing over the salmon and vegetables and garnish with fresh dill, a squeeze of lemon, and some cracked black pepper.

TIPS & NOTES

- *Some of my other favorite vegetables to include in this sheet pan meal are sliced mushrooms, asparagus spears, green beans, cauliflower florets, and fingerling potatoes.*

- *I like to serve the salmon and vegetables alongside a fluffy grain like quinoa, farro, or wild rice.*

CRAB and SHRIMP–STUFFED SALMON with CAPER-DILL HOLLANDAISE

SERVES: **6**

PREP TIME: **20 MINUTES**

COOK TIME: **30 MINUTES**

6 (6-ounce) salmon fillets, skin removed

1 tablespoon olive oil

Sea salt and black pepper

½ cup (4 ounces) cream cheese, softened

3 tablespoons mayonnaise

3 tablespoons heavy cream

1 tablespoon Worcestershire sauce

1 tablespoon Dijon mustard

2 teaspoons grated lemon zest

1 tablespoon fresh lemon juice

3 cloves garlic, minced

2 tablespoons chopped fresh dill

1 tablespoon chopped fresh chives

1 tablespoon dried minced onion

1 (10-ounce) package frozen spinach, thawed, drained, and squeezed dry

6 ounces jumbo lump crab meat

½ cup bay shrimp

4 tablespoons panko breadcrumbs, divided

4 tablespoons finely grated Parmesan cheese, divided

Caper-Dill Hollandaise (page 303), for serving

1. Preheat the oven to 400°F. Line a sheet pan with parchment paper.

2. Place the salmon fillets on the prepared pan. Using a sharp knife, slice down the middle of each fillet, creating a pocket and making sure that the knife does not go all the way through; leave the salmon flesh intact at the bottom and on both ends. Brush the salmon with the olive oil and season generously with salt and pepper.

3. Make the stuffing: In a large bowl, mix the cream cheese, mayonnaise, cream, Worcestershire, mustard, and lemon zest and juice until smooth. Stir in the garlic, dill, chives, dried onion, 1 teaspoon of salt, and ½ teaspoon of pepper until well combined. Fold in the spinach, crab meat, shrimp, 2 tablespoons of the panko, and 2 tablespoons of the Parmesan until well combined. Divide the mixture evenly among the salmon fillets, stuffing it into the pockets.

4. Bake for 10 minutes, or until the salmon has almost reached the desired doneness.

5. Increase the oven temperature to broil. Sprinkle the salmon with the remaining 2 tablespoons of panko and 2 tablespoons of Parmesan. Broil until the topping begins to brown. Drizzle some of the hollandaise over each fillet and serve the remainder on the side.

TIPS & NOTES

- *If you have stuffing left over, it is excellent topped with some mozzarella and Parmesan cheese, baked, and then served as a hot dip with crostini, chips, or vegetables.*

- *For gluten-free stuffed salmon, simply substitute your favorite gluten-free breadcrumbs, crushed pork rinds, or extra Parmesan cheese for the panko.*

- *I like to serve this dish with a hearty salad and my Umami Brussels Sprouts (page 259).*

CHICKEN TACOS

SERVES: **4**

PREP TIME: **25 MINUTES**

COOK TIME: **25 MINUTES**

2 tablespoons olive oil

4 (6-ounce) boneless, skinless chicken breasts (about 1½ pounds)

2 tablespoons Taco Seasoning (page 315)

3 cups shredded green cabbage

3 cups shredded purple cabbage

1 medium carrot, shredded or julienned

½ small red onion, thinly sliced

1 batch Cilantro-Lime Avocado Dressing (page 300)

FOR TOPPING/SERVING

1 large avocado, peeled, pitted, and diced

1 cup Cotija cheese

¼ cup seeded and chopped jalapeño

Chopped fresh cilantro

Tortillas, warmed

Lime wedges

1. Preheat the oven to 400°F. Line a sheet pan with parchment paper.

2. Brush the olive oil over the chicken breasts on both sides and season generously with the taco seasoning. Arrange the chicken on the prepared pan and bake for 20 to 25 minutes, until it is cooked through (165°F internal temperature).

3. While the chicken cooks, prepare the slaw: In a large mixing bowl, toss the cabbages, carrot, onion, and ½ cup of the dressing until the slaw is evenly coated.

4. Let the chicken rest for 5 minutes, then slice into strips. Divide the slaw among four serving bowls and arrange the chicken on top. Top with the avocado, Cotija, jalapeño, and cilantro. Drizzle the remaining dressing over the ingredients. Serve with warmed tortillas and lime wedges.

TIPS & NOTES

- *To save time (and money), you can substitute bagged coleslaw mix for the shredded cabbage and carrots. You will likely need two bags, depending on size. Discard any dressing that comes with it or save it for another use.*

- *Serve leftovers over rice for delicious chicken taco bowls.*

- *Swap out the chicken for shrimp, cod, halibut, or even steak.*

- *Entertaining? Turn this into a DIY taco bar by serving the sliced chicken, slaw, and dressing with different salsas, cheeses, chips, tortillas, beans, and rice.*

GNOCCHI with PANCETTA and VEGETABLES

SERVES: **4**

PREP TIME: **20 MINUTES**

COOK TIME: **20 MINUTES**

1 (20-ounce) package potato gnocchi

8 ounces pancetta, diced

1 large sweet potato (about 1 pound), peeled and cubed

1 small head broccoli (about 1 pound), cut into small florets

1 pint grape tomatoes

1 medium red onion, halved and sliced ½ inch thick

⅓ cup olive oil, plus extra for drizzling

2 tablespoons balsamic vinegar

¼ cup finely grated Parmesan cheese, plus extra for serving

5 cloves garlic, minced

1½ teaspoons finely chopped fresh sage

1½ teaspoons finely chopped fresh rosemary

1 teaspoon sea salt

½ teaspoon black pepper

Pinch of red pepper flakes

1. Preheat the oven to 450°F. Line a sheet pan with parchment paper.

2. Combine the gnocchi, pancetta, sweet potato, broccoli florets, tomatoes, and onion in a large mixing bowl. In a separate bowl, whisk together the olive oil, balsamic, Parmesan, garlic, sage, rosemary, salt, pepper, and red pepper flakes until all of the ingredients are well incorporated.

3. Pour the olive oil mixture over the gnocchi and vegetables and toss until everything is evenly coated. Spread in a single layer on the prepared pan.

4. Bake for 20 minutes, or until the gnocchi and sweet potatoes are tender and the tomatoes are blistered. Finish by drizzling a little olive oil over the top. Serve with extra Parmesan on the side.

TIPS & NOTES

- *In place of the pancetta, you can also use bacon, prosciutto, or even crumbled sausage.*

- *This is a great dish to mix and match any of your favorite vegetables or anything you have on hand that needs to be used up. Just make sure they are cut into uniformly sized pieces so that they cook evenly. Some of my other favorite vegetables to use in this dish are Brussels sprouts, zucchini, mushrooms, and butternut squash.*

- *Got leftovers? See page 337 for some delicious ideas.*

CUBAN POTATO SKINS

6 small (6-ounce) russet potatoes

2 tablespoons avocado oil

Sea salt

¼ cup salted butter, melted

2 tablespoons Dijon mustard

2 teaspoons Worcestershire sauce

1½ teaspoons garlic powder

1 cup shredded Swiss cheese, divided

6 slices Black Forest ham, cut in half, warmed

1 cup Pulled Pork (page 181), warmed

Sliced cornichons or small dill pickles, for garnish

Chopped fresh chives, for garnish

1. Preheat the oven to 425°F.

2. Scrub the potatoes and pierce each one multiple times with a fork. Rub the potatoes with the avocado oil and season generously with salt. Place the potatoes on a sheet pan and bake for 40 minutes, or until tender when poked with a fork. When cool enough to handle, cut them in half lengthwise. Use a spoon to scoop out the cooked potato, leaving a ¼- to ½-inch-thick shell.

3. In a small bowl, combine the melted butter, mustard, Worcestershire, and garlic powder. Brush the insides and outsides of the potato halves with half of the butter mixture.

4. Place the potatoes cut side down on the sheet pan and bake for 15 minutes. Flip the potatoes over and bake for an additional 5 minutes, or until slightly browned with crispy edges. Top the potato halves with ⅔ cup of the Swiss cheese. Return the potatoes to the oven and bake for 5 to 7 minutes more, until the cheese is melted and bubbly.

5. Fold a piece of ham on top of each potato half and top with some pulled pork. Sprinkle with the remaining ⅓ cup of Swiss cheese. Return the potatoes to the oven and bake until the cheese on top is melted and bubbly. Garnish with pickle slices and chives. Drizzle a small amount of the remaining melted butter mixture over the top of each potato half and serve the remaining butter on the side.

TIPS & NOTES

- *Gruyère, provolone, and sharp white cheddar are all great substitutions if you don't have Swiss. Even better, try a combination of the three.*

- *Instead of cornichons, you can use regular dill pickles, bread and butter pickles, or even pickled jalapeños for a bit of heat.*

- *If Dijon isn't your thing, yellow mustard, honey mustard, or stone-ground mustard all work well.*

- *To add a little kick, mix a bit of hot sauce or smoked paprika into the mustard-butter mixture.*

UPSIDE-DOWN CARAMELIZED SHALLOT and BRIE TARTS

SERVES: **4**

PREP TIME: **20 MINUTES**

COOK TIME: **25 MINUTES**

1 sheet frozen puff pastry dough (half of a 17-ounce package), thawed

1 tablespoon olive oil

1 tablespoon balsamic vinegar

Sea salt

Cracked black pepper

A few sprigs fresh thyme, plus extra for garnish

2 cloves garlic, thinly sliced

2 medium shallots, peeled and thinly sliced from root to tip

1 (8-ounce) wheel Brie cheese, cut into 8 equal slices

1 large egg

1 teaspoon water

Hot honey, for serving

Red pepper flakes, for garnish

1. Preheat the oven to 350°F. Line a sheet pan with parchment paper.

2. Roll out the pastry sheet and cut into 8 equal-size rectangles. Set the pastry aside.

3. Map out where you will put each piece of pastry dough on the prepared pan; you may need to use two pans. Drizzle a little olive oil and balsamic vinegar where you will place each piece of dough. Sprinkle salt, pepper, thyme, and garlic slices over the olive oil and balsamic vinegar. Arrange a few slices of shallot on top of each pile, then top each with a slice of Brie. Place a piece of pastry dough on top of each of the piles. Use a fork to crimp the edges all around each piece.

4. In a small bowl, whisk together the egg and water. Brush the top of each tart with the egg wash. Bake the pastries for 25 minutes, or until golden brown. Let cool for 5 minutes before removing from the parchment paper. You may need to carefully slide a spatula underneath to help release them.

5. Drizzle the tops with a little hot honey and garnish with a pinch of red pepper flakes and thyme.

> **TIPS & NOTES**
>
> - *Puff pastry is best worked with while still cold but not frozen. If it gets too soft, pop it back in the fridge for 10 minutes to firm up before baking.*
>
> - *Other delicious cheese options are Camembert, Cambozola, smoked Gouda, goat cheese, or even Gruyère.*
>
> - *Add a few slices of ripe pear or apple under the Brie for a sweet and savory twist.*

BAKED HEIRLOOM CAPRESE with WARM BACON VINAIGRETTE

SERVES: **4**

PREP TIME: **15 MINUTES**

COOK TIME: **25 MINUTES**

6 slices bacon

2 pounds heirloom tomatoes, cut into ½-inch-thick slices

3 cloves garlic, thinly sliced

3 tablespoons balsamic vinegar

2 tablespoons olive oil

12 ounces fresh mozzarella cheese, cut into ¼-inch-thick slices

Sea salt and black pepper

15 fresh basil leaves, for garnish

1. Preheat the oven to 300°F. Line a sheet pan with parchment paper.

2. Cook the bacon in a large skillet over medium heat until crispy. Transfer to paper towels to remove the excess grease and cool slightly. Save the bacon drippings for the vinaigrette. Crumble the bacon and set aside.

3. Line the tomato slices in a single layer on the prepared sheet pan and top with the garlic. Bake for 20 to 25 minutes, until the tomatoes are warm and tender but not mushy.

4. Make the vinaigrette: In a small mixing bowl, whisk together 3 tablespoons of the reserved bacon drippings, the balsamic vinegar, and olive oil.

5. Top the tomatoes with the mozzarella slices and crumbled bacon and drizzle the vinaigrette over everything. Sprinkle with a little salt and pepper, garnish with fresh basil leaves, and serve.

> **TIPS & NOTES**
>
> - *Keep an eye on the tomatoes as they roast. Softer varieties like heirlooms cook faster, so adjust your timing to ensure they don't collapse completely (unless you love a jammy texture).*
>
> - *To turn this into a deconstructed BLT bruschetta, serve it over crusty toasted bread with some mayo and mixed greens.*
>
> - *Pair with a chilled glass of crisp white wine, such as Sauvignon Blanc or Pinot Grigio.*
>
> - *For a vegetarian option, swap out the crumbled bacon for toasted pine nuts, crispy shallots, or thin slices of roasted mushrooms. Replace the bacon drippings with melted butter.*

CHEESY GARLIC ROASTED ASPARAGUS

SERVES: 4

PREP TIME: **15 MINUTES**

COOK TIME: **15 MINUTES**

1 pound asparagus spears, ends trimmed

2 tablespoons olive oil

4 cloves garlic, minced

¾ teaspoon sea salt

¾ cup shredded mozzarella cheese

¾ cup shredded smoked white cheddar cheese

Cracked black pepper

1. Preheat the oven to 425°F.

2. Arrange the asparagus in a single layer on a sheet pan. Drizzle the olive oil over the asparagus and sprinkle with the garlic and salt. Toss to evenly coat the spears, then spread them back out in a nice even layer. Bake for 10 minutes, or until the asparagus is just starting to get tender but is still a vibrant green.

3. Top with the mozzarella and cheddar. Increase the oven temperature to high broil and broil until the cheese is golden brown and bubbling, about 5 minutes.

4. Top with cracked black pepper before serving. Taste and add more salt, if desired.

TIPS & NOTES

- *You can use any cheeses you prefer here. One of my other favorite pairings is Parmesan and pepper jack: Parmesan adds a nice nuttiness, while pepper jack contributes a little kick.*

- *Make it a full meal deal by adding bite-size pieces of chicken breast. Just double the amount of olive oil and salt and toss the chicken in with the asparagus. Sprinkle it all with crumbled bacon.*

CRISPY GARLIC CHICKPEAS

SERVES: 4

PREP TIME: **10 MINUTES**

COOK TIME: **20 MINUTES**

2 (15-ounce) cans chickpeas, drained and rinsed

2 teaspoons garlic powder

½ teaspoon onion powder

½ teaspoon smoked paprika

½ teaspoon sea salt

½ teaspoon black pepper

2 tablespoons avocado oil

1. Preheat the oven to 400°F.

2. Blot the drained and rinsed chickpeas dry with paper towels. The drier you get them, the crispier they will turn out.

3. In a small bowl, whisk together the garlic powder, onion powder, paprika, salt, and pepper until well incorporated.

4. In a bowl, toss the chickpeas with the avocado oil and spice mixture until evenly coated. Spread the chickpeas in a single layer on a sheet pan. Bake for 10 minutes and toss. Bake for 10 minutes longer, or until browned and crunchy.

5. Store leftovers in an airtight container at room temperature for up to 2 weeks.

TIPS & NOTES

- *Enjoy these chickpeas on their own for a protein-packed snack.*

- *Sprinkle on top of a salad—like my Kale, Spinach, and Romaine Caesar (page 207)—for added crunch.*

- *Add to toast recipes, like Caesar Salad Breakfast Toast (page 233), Dill Egg Salad Toast (page 234), or Smoked Salmon Toast (page 237).*

30-MINUTE
RECIPES

Some days, cooking feels like a self-care ritual—a slow, deliberate process done with intention that nourishes body, mind, and spirit. Other days, life is coming at you full speed, you've barely had time to take a breath all day, and spending time in the kitchen feels like torture.

Enter the gift of 30-minute recipes: dishes that are satisfying and flavorful without demanding hours of dicing, chopping, simmering, and sweating over a hot stove.

The key to making a meal, start to finish, in 30 minutes or less is efficiency. In this chapter, I'll teach you how to streamline your cooking process and elevate everyday ingredients into something special to make every minute count—all with minimal effort.

COOKING TECHNIQUES

Understanding a few key cooking techniques can make all the difference when you're aiming to prepare a meal in under 30 minutes. High-heat methods like grilling, pan-searing, stir-frying, and roasting are perfect for quick, flavorful dishes. These techniques not only speed up cooking time but also lock in deep, bold flavors.

Grilling and pan-searing are fantastic for proteins, as the intense heat creates a perfectly seared crust while cooking the food quickly. Whether it's steak, chicken thighs, or fish fillets, both grilling and searing allow you to cook to completion in just a handful of minutes without sacrificing moisture or flavor.

The same goes for stir-frying, which is ideal when you're working with smaller, uniformly cut ingredients like chopped meats and vegetables. Stir-frying at high heat in a wok or skillet ensures that the ingredients cook evenly and rapidly while still maintaining their vibrant color and fresh texture.

Roasting is another high-heat method that can speed up cooking. The key is preheating your oven to a high temperature, usually around 400°F, so that the food cooks quickly and develops that irresistibly caramelized exterior. For example, roasting a tray of chopped vegetables at this temperature will result in crispy, perfectly charred edges.

Lastly, don't underestimate the power of a simple sauté. This is one of the fastest ways to cook proteins and vegetables. All you need is a hot pan with a small amount of fat to cook food quickly while enhancing flavor and preserving texture. Shrimp, fish, chicken, pork, and beef all benefit from a quick sauté, and by adding aromatics like fresh herbs, garlic, shallots, or ginger, you'll be well on your way to a dish that is both quick and loaded with flavor.

MISE EN PLACE

Efficiency in the kitchen is just as much about preparation as it is about technique. I am a firm believer that, if someone says they don't enjoy cooking, I can easily change their mind by teaching them how to be more efficient in the kitchen.

The French term *mise en place* literally means "everything in its place." It's one of the most beneficial habits for a stress-free, streamlined cooking experience. (A very close second is cleaning as you go.) When you have all your ingredients and tools prepped and organized, cooking becomes a much easier and more fulfilling process.

As soon as you walk into the kitchen, take a few minutes to gather and prep your ingredients and all necessary pans and cooking utensils. If you are using a recipe, pull it out and read it in its entirety so that there are no surprises along the way. Chop and portion out vegetables, measure out spices, oils, and vinegars, and make sure your proteins are cleaned, trimmed, and ready to go.

> **PRO TIP:**
>
> *This level of organization can also extend to how you store your ingredients. If you know that throughout the week or during a day of meal prep, you are going to use chopped onions, diced bell peppers, sliced carrots, sliced celery, and minced garlic, you can cut them all down at once and store them in individual containers. It makes the actual cooking process that much faster.*

MULTITASKING

In addition to *mise en place*, when cooking multiple recipes at once, the ability to efficiently multitask becomes very important. Kitchen multitasking—cooking multiple components of a recipe at once, or cooking multiple recipes at once—is also a powerful tool in your efficiency arsenal. While pasta is boiling, sauté vegetables in another pan. While chicken sears in a skillet, get started on a pot of homemade sauce. While vegetables are roasting in the oven, cook salmon in the air fryer. The key is to make sure that you're using your time wisely. Efficiency is also about making good use of hands-off time during the cooking process. For example: If your recipe calls for rice, consider preparing it in a rice cooker or a pressure cooker while you work on other parts of the meal—the rice will take care of itself and free up your time and focus for the more hands-on parts of the meal.

Similarly, when roasting and baking, try to cook as much as possible in one go. For example, put a batch of vegetables in the oven for tomorrow's lunch while you're making tonight's main protein. Batch-cooking ensures that you have leftovers that can be repurposed for any meal later in the week. This approach not only saves you time in the long run but also helps you avoid the need for multiple rounds of cleanup. "Cook once, eat multiple times" is always my motto.

> **NOTE:**
>
> *Some of the recipes in this chapter, such as the Balsamic Pesto Beef Kabobs (page 96) and the Chili-Lime Flank Steak with Grilled Corn Salsa (page 98) do require extra time for marinating. This is the perfect example of something you can do ahead of time, or even the day before to streamline the cooking process at mealtime. Alternatively, you can cook immediately without marinating, but the end result might not be as flavorful.*

TOOLS AND GADGETS

The right tools can make all the difference when it comes to speeding up the cooking process. A few essential gadgets are worth investing in to make 30-minute meals even easier to execute. My favorite thing about 30-minute meals is that they aren't exclusive to any one cooking method. Some sheet pan meals, air fryer meals, and even one-pot meals can be completed in less than 30 minutes.

Quality pans: Don't underestimate the value of a quality nonstick pan. This is an area where you truly get what you pay for. A good set of pans, if cared for properly, could easily outlive you. My favorites are enameled cast-iron and HexClad pans. Just make sure to avoid any type of nonstick cookware with Teflon or some other poorly made, cheap nonstick coating.

Sheet pans: A large sheet pan (a baking sheet that has a rim to catch liquids and keep food from sliding off) is one of the most versatile pans in your kitchen. From baking cookies to roasting a big tray of vegetables to cooking a complete meal, a set of sheet pans makes for quick and delicious meals and easy cleanup—especially when lined with parchment paper.

Knives: A good chef's knife allows you to chop, slice, and dice with precision and speed, helping cut down on prep time. A sharp knife is a safe knife—more kitchen accidents happen with a dull knife as opposed to a sharp one. Some of my favorite knife brands are Global, Wüsthof, and HexClad.

Food processor and blender: Food processors, high-powered blenders, and immersion blenders can significantly reduce the amount of time spent dicing, chopping, mincing, slicing, and mixing. A food processor can mince garlic, chop onions, and even shred cheese in seconds. A blender purees soups and blends sauces and dressings with minimal time and effort, while an immersion blender is perfect for shortcut blending right on the stovetop.

Small tools: Even gadgets as simple as citrus juicers, Microplanes, and garlic presses can save time and help you extract every last bit of flavor and value from your ingredients.

Ultimately, 30-minute recipes are about making the most of what you've got, in terms of both time and ingredients, to create a satisfying and nourishing meal. With the right techniques and equipment, some thoughtful organization, and a dash of creativity, you can be in and out of the kitchen in no time. So, roll up your sleeves and let's get cooking. I think you'll be amazed at how much you can do in a short time.

GARLIC BUTTER STEAK BITES

SERVES: **8**

PREP TIME: **15 MINUTES**

COOK TIME: **10 MINUTES**

3 pounds beef tenderloin, cut into bite-sized pieces

1 head garlic, cloves peeled and thinly sliced

⅓ cup tamari or soy sauce

2 tablespoons dried minced onion

1 tablespoon chopped fresh oregano

1 tablespoon chopped fresh flat-leaf parsley, plus extra for garnish

1½ teaspoons chopped fresh thyme

2 teaspoons smoked paprika

1 teaspoon garlic powder

1 teaspoon sea salt

½ teaspoon black pepper

2 tablespoons olive oil

½ cup (1 stick) salted butter

1. In a large mixing bowl, combine the beef, garlic, tamari, dried onion, oregano, parsley, thyme, paprika, garlic powder, salt, and pepper. Toss to coat, making sure that all of the pieces of the meat are evenly coated. If time allows, refrigerate for 2 hours or up to 24 hours. This allows the flavors to come together and penetrate the meat.

2. Heat the olive oil in a large skillet over medium-high heat. Add the steak bites to the pan and sear on all sides, 2 to 3 minutes on each side. If you do not have a large pan, you may need to do this in batches to prevent overcrowding.

3. Once the steak bites are nice and seared and have formed a slight crust, add the butter and toss the steak in the butter as it melts. Garnish with the reserved parsley and serve.

TIPS & NOTES

- *If you have a pellet smoker, this is a perfect recipe to smoke. It's simple, too: Just heat your smoker to 225°F. Spread the marinated beef in a single layer across a sheet pan, top with the butter, and let it melt into the meat. Smoke for about 1 hour, until the internal temperature of the meat reaches 135°F, tossing the steak bites in the butter a few times as it cooks.*

- *To substitute dried herbs for the fresh, simply reduce the amount by two-thirds. For example, 1 tablespoon of fresh herbs can be substituted with 1 teaspoon of dried herbs.*

BALSAMIC PESTO BEEF KABOBS

SERVES: **4**

PREP TIME: **20 MINUTES, PLUS TIME TO MARINATE**

COOK TIME: **10 MINUTES**

FOR THE BALSAMIC PESTO VINAIGRETTE

1 cup avocado oil or extra-virgin olive oil

½ cup balsamic vinegar

¼ cup pesto

2 tablespoons Dijon mustard

2 tablespoons fresh lemon juice

2 cloves garlic, grated on a Microplane, or 1 tablespoon plus 1 teaspoon dried minced garlic

1 teaspoon red pepper flakes

1 teaspoon onion powder

1 teaspoon sea salt

FOR THE KABOBS

2 pounds top sirloin steak, cut into large chunks

1 large red bell pepper, seeded and cut into large chunks

1 large green bell pepper, seeded and cut into large chunks

1 large zucchini, cut into ½-inch-thick slices

1 large summer squash, cut into ½-inch-thick slices

1 small red onion, cut into large chunks

1 small sweet potato, halved lengthwise and cut into ½-inch-thick slices

15 large button mushrooms, halved

Cracked black pepper

SPECIAL EQUIPMENT:

8 to 10 (12-inch) skewers

1. Make the vinaigrette: In a bowl, whisk together all of the ingredients.

2. In a large mixing bowl, combine the steak, bell peppers, zucchini, summer squash, red onion, sweet potato, mushrooms, and cracked black pepper. Add the vinaigrette and toss until the meat and vegetables are thoroughly coated. Refrigerate for 3 to 4 hours or up to overnight.

3. Preheat a grill to medium heat (about 350°F). Oil the grill grates.

4. Alternating ingredients, thread the beef and vegetables onto skewers. Grill, turning halfway through cooking, until the meat has reached the desired level of doneness and the vegetables are charred and softened.

TIPS & NOTES

• *Swap out the sirloin chunks for chicken breast or shrimp—or even tofu for a vegetarian twist. Adjust the grilling time accordingly.*

• *If you don't have skewers, grill the meat and veggies in a grill basket for an equally delicious dish.*

• *If using wooden skewers, make sure to soak them in water for 30 minutes before grilling so that they do not catch on fire.*

CHILI-LIME FLANK STEAK with GRILLED CORN SALSA

FOR THE FLANK STEAK

2 tablespoons olive oil

3 cloves garlic, minced

1½ packed tablespoons brown sugar

1 tablespoon chili powder

2 teaspoons sea salt

1½ teaspoons ground cumin

1 teaspoon black pepper

1 teaspoon smoked paprika

Pinch of red pepper flakes

Grated zest and juice of 1 lime

1½ to 2 pounds flank steak

FOR THE GRILLED CORN SALSA

6 ears yellow corn, shucked

4 tablespoons olive oil, divided

Sea salt and black pepper

Grated zest and juice of 1 lime

2 cloves garlic, minced

½ teaspoon ground cumin

2 vine-ripened tomatoes, diced

1 small red bell pepper, seeded and diced

1 jalapeño, seeded and finely chopped

½ cup crumbled Cotija cheese

½ cup diced red onion

¼ cup chopped fresh cilantro

FOR GARNISH/SERVING

Lime wedges

Fresh cilantro

Tortilla chips

Guacamole

1. In a small bowl, whisk together the olive oil, garlic, brown sugar, chili powder, salt, cumin, black pepper, paprika, red pepper flakes, and lime zest and juice. Place the steak on a sheet pan or in a large casserole dish. Pour half of the marinade onto one side and pat it into the meat. Flip the steak over and do the same thing on the other side. Marinate in the refrigerator for 6 hours or up to overnight.

2. Let the steak come to room temperature. Preheat a grill to medium-high heat (375°F to 400°F). Oil the grill grates.

3. Remove the steak from the marinade. Place on the grill, close the lid, and cook for 7 to 8 minutes. Flip and cook for an additional 5 to 6 minutes on the other side, until the internal temperature of the meat reaches 130°F to 135°F for medium-rare to medium. Let the steak rest for 10 minutes, then thinly slice at a slight angle, against the grain.

4. Meanwhile, brush the ears of corn with 2 tablespoons of the olive oil and season generously with salt and pepper. Grill, turning every few minutes, until golden with slight char marks and cooked through, about 12 minutes. Let cool, then cut the kernels off the cobs.

5. In a small bowl, whisk together the remaining 2 tablespoons of olive oil, the lime zest and juice, garlic, and cumin. In a large mixing bowl, toss the corn, tomatoes, bell pepper, jalapeño, Cotija, onion, and cilantro. Drizzle the oil mixture over the vegetables and toss again until the corn salad is evenly coated. Taste and add more salt and pepper, if desired.

6. Plate the flank steak and top with the corn salsa. Garnish with cilantro and serve with lime wedges, tortilla chips, and guacamole.

TIPS & NOTES

This recipe has a lot of ingredients, but it comes together quickly. To save time, prep the salsa ingredients while the meat and corn are on the grill.

SLOPPY MACS

1½ pounds ground beef

2 tablespoons dried minced onion

2 cloves garlic, minced

1 tablespoon Worcestershire sauce

Sea salt and black pepper, to taste

2 batches Burger Sauce (page 305)

4 large sesame seed hamburger buns

1 small head iceberg lettuce, finely shredded

4 slices American cheese

16 dill pickle slices

1. In a large skillet over medium heat, cook the ground beef, dried onion, garlic, Worcestershire sauce, and salt and pepper until the beef is fully browned, 8 to 10 minutes. Drain any excess grease. Mix 1¼ cups of the burger sauce into the meat mixture.

2. Split each of the buns. Spread a little bit of burger sauce on each of the bottom buns, then top with lettuce. Divide the meat mixture evenly among all four bottom buns and top with a slice of cheese, then four pickle chips. Drizzle some sauce over each, put on the top buns, and serve.

TIPS & NOTES

- *Make these double decker style by adding an extra bottom bun layer in the middle, just like a Big Mac.*

- *For added texture and to keep the buns from getting soggy, I like to toast them in a pan with a little butter before assembling.*

COPYCAT HAMBURGER HELPER BEEF STROGANOFF

12 ounces casarecce pasta

2 tablespoons olive oil

1 small yellow onion, diced

4 cloves garlic, minced

1 pound ground beef

2 tablespoons Worcestershire sauce

6 ounces shiitake mushrooms, thinly sliced

1½ teaspoons sea salt

1 teaspoon garlic powder

1 teaspoon onion powder

1 teaspoon smoked paprika

½ teaspoon ground black pepper

1 cup beef stock

1½ cups sour cream

Finely chopped fresh flat-leaf parsley, for garnish

1. Cook the pasta per the package directions until al dente; drain and set aside.

2. While the pasta is cooking, heat the olive oil in a large skillet over medium-low heat. Add the onion and cook until soft and translucent, about 5 minutes. Add the garlic and cook until fragrant, about 2 minutes. Add the ground beef, breaking it up as it cooks, until browned, about 8 minutes. Drain any excess grease.

3. Add the Worcestershire sauce, mushrooms, salt, garlic powder, onion powder, paprika, and pepper and cook until the mushrooms are tender, about 6 minutes.

4. Add the stock and sour cream and mix until well combined. Bring to a slow boil, then reduce the heat to a simmer. Simmer until the sauce has thickened. Taste and add more salt and pepper, if desired.

5. Add the cooked pasta to the pan and toss until evenly coated in the sauce. Garnish with parsley before serving.

TIPS & NOTES

- *Casarecce pasta (a short, twisted pasta with a slightly rolled, tube-like shape and an open groove down the center) holds the sauce well, but you can also use egg noodles, penne, or rotini.*

- *To keep the sour cream from curdling, ensure that the heat is low when adding it and stir continuously.*

- *Swap out the sour cream for Greek yogurt for a slightly tangier, protein-packed alternative.*

REUBEN EGG ROLLS

SERVES: **4**

PREP TIME: **15 MINUTES**

COOK TIME: **10 MINUTES**

1 pound corned beef, shredded and chopped

½ cup shredded Gruyère cheese

½ cup shredded Swiss cheese

¾ cup sauerkraut, rinsed and drained

½ teaspoon caraway seeds

12 egg roll wrappers

1 large egg, whisked

Canola or vegetable oil, for frying

Russian Dressing (page 304), for serving

1. Put the corned beef, cheeses, sauerkraut, and caraway seeds in a large mixing bowl and mix until the ingredients are well combined.

2. Lay out the egg roll wrappers in a single layer. Brush the edges of each with a light coating of the whisked egg. Divide the filling evenly among the wrappers, spreading it out in the middle of each. With the point of the wrapper facing toward you, tightly fold both sides of the wrapper inward, then roll up (like you are folding a burrito) to enclose the filling. Seal the edges with more egg or with a little bit of water. Repeat to make 12 egg rolls.

3. In a high-sided skillet or Dutch oven, heat 1 inch of oil over medium-high heat. (If using a thermometer, heat to 350°F.) In batches of three or four egg rolls, fry for 1 to 2 minutes on each side, until golden brown all over. Remove the egg rolls from the oil and place on a paper towel to absorb the excess oil.

4. Cut the egg rolls in half, slicing on a bias. Serve with Russian dressing on the side.

FLAVOR VARIATIONS

- **Cuban Egg Rolls:** *Replace the corned beef with roasted pork and add ham, Swiss cheese, pickles, and a swipe of yellow mustard.*

- **Philly Cheesesteak Egg Rolls:** *Use thinly sliced steak, provolone cheese, and sautéed onions and peppers.*

- **Buffalo Reuben Egg Rolls:** *Add a drizzle of buffalo sauce to the filling and serve with blue cheese dressing.*

- **German-Style Egg Rolls:** *Swap out the cheeses for smoked cheddar and add a little stone-ground mustard to the filling. Serve with a warm beer cheese dip.*

- **Breakfast Egg Rolls:** *Add scrambled eggs, hash browns, and corned beef or pastrami. Serve with hollandaise (see Tips & Notes in the Caper-Dill Hollandaise recipe, page 303).*

EGG ROLL BURGERS

FOR THE BURGERS

1½ pounds ground pork

½ small white onion, grated on a Microplane

3 cloves garlic, grated on a Microplane

1 tablespoon soy sauce

1½ teaspoons ground ginger

1½ teaspoons unseasoned rice vinegar

1 teaspoon chili paste or sriracha

½ teaspoon sea salt

½ teaspoon black pepper

1 tablespoon toasted sesame oil

4 large sesame seed hamburger buns

2 tablespoons salted butter

FOR THE COLESLAW

8 ounces coleslaw mix (with green and purple cabbage and carrots)

3 green onions, thinly sliced

1 batch Yum Yum Sauce (page 306)

1. Put the ground pork, onion, garlic, soy sauce, ginger, rice vinegar, chili paste, salt, and pepper in a large mixing bowl and mix with your hands until the ingredients are well incorporated. Form the mixture into four equal-sized patties, about ½ inch thick. Use your thumb to press a well into the center of each patty. (This will help them cook evenly and keep them from plumping up too much in the center.)

2. Heat the sesame oil in a large skillet over medium-high heat. Once the pan is hot and the oil is shimmering, place the pork patties in the pan and cook until they are nice and caramelized and cooked all the way through, 6 to 7 minutes on each side.

3. While the burgers are cooking, combine the coleslaw mix and green onions in a large mixing bowl. Add yum yum sauce to coat, reserving some sauce to spread on the buns.

4. Preheat a separate skillet over medium heat. Butter the cut sides of the buns. Place, buttered side down, in the pan and toast for 2 to 3 minutes, until the buns are golden brown. Spread a little sauce on each of the bottom buns and top with a pork burger, then a heaping mound of the coleslaw. Drizzle a little more sauce over the slaw, then add the top buns.

> **TIPS & NOTES**
>
> - *Add pickled ginger, sliced cucumber, or a fried egg for a gourmet twist.*
>
> - *For a low-carb option, skip the buns and serve the pork patties over a bed of the coleslaw, drizzling yum yum sauce on top.*
>
> - *The pork patties can be mixed and shaped up to 24 hours ahead. Keep them covered in the fridge until ready to cook.*

PARMESAN-CRUSTED CHICKEN with LEMON CREAM SAUCE

SERVES: **2**

PREP TIME: **10 MINUTES**

COOK TIME: **20 MINUTES**

FOR THE SAUCE

1 cup heavy cream

2 cloves garlic, minced

2 tablespoons fresh lemon juice

1 teaspoon lemon pepper seasoning

½ cup finely grated Parmesan cheese

FOR THE CHICKEN

1 large egg

½ cup finely grated Parmesan cheese

2 teaspoons Italian seasoning

2 tablespoons olive oil

1 pound boneless, skinless chicken breasts, thinly sliced into cutlets

1. Make the sauce: In a small saucepan over medium heat, combine the cream, garlic, lemon juice, and lemon pepper seasoning. Slowly bring to a gentle boil, then reduce the heat to low. Once the sauce starts to simmer and has small bubbles at the edge of the pan, add the Parmesan. Mix until the cheese is melted and incorporated into the sauce. Continue to simmer, stirring occasionally, while you prepare the chicken.

2. Set up two shallow bowls: In one bowl, whisk the egg with a fork to make an egg wash. In the second bowl, combine the Parmesan and Italian seasoning. Coat each chicken cutlet with the egg wash and then liberally coat with the Parmesan mixture.

3. Heat the olive oil in a large skillet over medium to medium-high heat. Add the chicken and cook for 5 minutes, or until crispy and golden brown on the bottom. Flip and cook for 3 to 5 minutes longer, until the other side is golden brown and crispy. (Flip the chicken only once during cooking to ensure that the breading stays on.)

4. Remove the chicken from the pan and top with the sauce.

TIPS & NOTES

- *Serve with Garlic-Herb Mashed Potatoes (page 189) drizzled with extra lemon cream sauce, along with Umami Brussels Sprouts (page 259).*

- *Spice things up by adding a little Blackened Seasoning (page 315) to the Parmesan coating.*

- *Instead of the fresh garlic, mash up some Garlic Confit (page 310) and mix it into the sauce to bring in more of a roasted, nutty flavor.*

- *For a crispier crust, replace half of the Parmesan with panko.*

CRISPY CHICKEN THIGH PICCATA

SERVES: **4**

PREP TIME: **10 MINUTES**

COOK TIME: **20 MINUTES**

8 bone-in, skin-on chicken thighs (about 1½ pounds)

2 teaspoons sea salt

1 teaspoon Italian seasoning

1 teaspoon garlic powder

½ teaspoon ground black pepper

2 tablespoons olive oil

3 tablespoons salted butter

3 tablespoons capers, drained

2 tablespoons fresh lemon juice

1 lemon, sliced into wheels

Chopped fresh flat-leaf parsley, for garnish

1. Preheat the oven to 400°F.

2. Season the chicken thighs generously on both sides with the salt, Italian seasoning, garlic powder, and pepper. Heat the olive oil in a large ovenproof skillet over medium-high heat. Add the chicken, skin side down, and cook for 5 minutes, or until the skin is nice and crispy.

3. Flip the thighs over, transfer the skillet to the oven, and bake for 15 to 20 minutes, until the chicken is cooked all the way through. Remove the chicken from the pan, set aside, and cover to keep warm.

4. To the same skillet, add the butter, capers, lemon juice, and lemon slices and use a rubber spatula to scrape up and mix in any bits stuck to the bottom of the pan. Plate the chicken and pour the sauce over the top. Garnish with parsley and serve.

TIPS & NOTES

- *Don't rush the sear. Let the thighs cook undisturbed before flipping. If they stick, they're not ready yet!*

- *I like to serve this over Garlic-Herb Mashed Potatoes (page 189) or with Cheesy Garlic Roasted Asparagus (page 83).*

LEMON-DILL CHICKEN with ARTICHOKES

SERVES: **4**

PREP TIME: **10 MINUTES**

COOK TIME: **20 MINUTES**

1½ pounds chicken cutlets

Sea salt and black pepper

1 teaspoon garlic powder

1 tablespoon olive oil

1 tablespoon salted butter

½ cup chicken stock

¾ cup heavy cream

2 tablespoons fresh lemon juice

1 teaspoon lemon pepper seasoning

¼ cup finely grated Parmesan cheese

1 (14-ounce) can quartered marinated artichoke hearts, drained

1 tablespoon chopped fresh dill, plus extra for garnish

1 small lemon, cut into wedges, for serving

1. Season the chicken cutlets generously on both sides with salt and pepper. Sprinkle the garlic powder over the top.

2. Heat the olive oil and butter in a large skillet over medium-high heat. Once the butter is melted into the oil, add the chicken cutlets and pan-sear until golden brown and cooked through, 3 to 4 minutes on each side. Remove the chicken from the pan, cover, and set aside.

3. Deglaze the pan with the stock, using a rubber spatula to scrape up and mix in any bits that are stuck to the bottom. Add the cream, lemon juice, and lemon pepper seasoning and bring to a boil. Reduce the heat to low and stir in the Parmesan cheese. Let simmer for 5 to 10 minutes, until the sauce has reduced a bit and started to thicken. Taste and add additional salt and pepper, if desired. Add the artichoke hearts and dill and cook for an additional 5 minutes.

4. Plate the chicken cutlets and pour the sauce over the top. Garnish with dill and serve with lemon wedges.

TIPS & NOTES

- *For an extra serving of vegetables, add baby spinach, peas, or halved cherry tomatoes during the last few minutes of cooking.*

- *Capers or a splash of white wine (in place of some of the chicken stock) can add an extra layer of brightness.*

- *No fresh dill? Fresh parsley or basil also works beautifully here.*

112   SIMPLY**DELICIOUS**

BLACKENED MAHI MAHI with PINEAPPLE SALSA

SERVES: **4**

PREP TIME: **15 MINUTES**

COOK TIME: **10 MINUTES**

FOR THE MAHI MAHI

4 (6-ounce) mahi mahi fillets

1 batch Blackened Seasoning (page 315)

2 tablespoons salted butter

1 tablespoon olive oil

FOR THE PINEAPPLE SALSA

1 medium pineapple, cored and cubed small

3 Roma tomatoes, cored and diced

2 cloves garlic, minced

1 jalapeño, seeded and finely chopped

½ cup diced mixed bell peppers

½ cup finely chopped red onion

3 tablespoons chopped fresh cilantro, or more to taste

Grated zest and juice of 1 lime

½ teaspoon sea salt

1 lime, cut into wedges, for serving

1. Pat the fish fillets dry with a paper towel. Season liberally on all sides with the blackened seasoning, pressing the seasoning into the fish.

2. Heat the butter and olive oil in a large skillet over medium-high heat. Once the butter is melted into the oil, add the seasoned fish and cook for 3 to 4 minutes, until a nice crust starts to form. Use a fish spatula to flip the fish over and cook until it is opaque on the other side and cooked all the way through, 2 to 3 minutes.

3. Make the salsa: Put all of the ingredients in a large mixing bowl and toss to combine.

4. Plate the blackened mahi mahi, top with the salsa, and serve with lime wedges.

> **TIPS & NOTES**
>
> - *Instead of mahi mahi, you can use halibut, snapper, cod, or even salmon.*
>
> - *Instead of pineapple, try mango or peaches—or both. For a shortcut, you can use canned pineapple.*

CHEESY SPINACH-STUFFED PEPPERS

SERVES: **4**

PREP TIME: **15 MINUTES**

COOK TIME: **30 MINUTES**

4 red bell peppers, halved vertically and seeded

2 tablespoons olive oil

1 large yellow onion, diced

4 cloves garlic, minced

4 cups fresh spinach, or 1 (14-ounce) package frozen spinach

1 teaspoon sea salt

½ teaspoon black pepper

⅛ teaspoon ground nutmeg

2½ cups shredded mozzarella cheese, divided

12 ounces ricotta cheese

1. Preheat the oven to 375°F.

2. Place the peppers cut side up in a baking dish and bake for 10 minutes, until crisp-tender.

3. While the peppers are in the oven, make the spinach stuffing: Heat the olive oil in a large skillet over medium heat. Add the onion and garlic and cook until the onion is translucent, about 8 minutes. Add the spinach, salt, pepper, and nutmeg and cook until the spinach is wilted. Reduce the heat to low and mix in 1½ cups of the mozzarella and the ricotta. Cook, stirring constantly, until the cheese is melted and creamy. Taste and add more salt and pepper, if desired.

4. Divide the stuffing mixture evenly among the bell pepper halves. Top with the remaining mozzarella. Bake for an additional 10 minutes, or until the cheese is brown and bubbly and the edges of the peppers are slightly charred.

TIPS & NOTES

- *Mix and match any of your favorite cheeses. Some of my other favorites to use here include sharp white cheddar, fontina, and Gouda.*

- *Add shrimp, ground turkey, chicken, or Italian sausage for a heartier, protein-packed filling.*

- *If using frozen spinach, you will want to thaw before using, then drain and squeeze dry.*

---

116   SIMPLY**DELICIOUS**

SIMPLE GRILLED VEGETABLES

SERVES: **4**

PREP TIME: **15 MINUTES**

COOK TIME: **15 MINUTES**

4 ears yellow corn, shucked

2 zucchinis, sliced lengthwise into ½-inch-thick planks

1 medium red onion, sliced into ⅓-inch-thick rounds

1 large red bell pepper, seeded and cut into large strips

1 large orange bell pepper, seeded and cut into large strips

3 tablespoons avocado oil or olive oil

1 teaspoon garlic powder

½ teaspoon onion powder

½ teaspoon dried oregano

Sea salt and black pepper

1. Line all of the vegetables in a single layer across a sheet pan. In a small bowl, whisk together the oil, garlic powder, onion powder, and oregano. Drizzle the oil mixture over the vegetables and toss to evenly coat. Season generously with salt and pepper.

2. Preheat a grill to medium heat (about 350°F). Lightly oil the grill grates.

3. Put the corn on the grill first and cook for 4 minutes on each side. Add the remaining vegetables and cook for 3 to 4 minutes on each side, until crisp-tender with char marks. Alternatively, you can cook all of the remaining vegetables in a grill basket for easy cleanup.

TIPS & NOTES

- *If you don't have a grill, you can cook the vegetables on a grill pan on the stovetop.*

- FLAVORFUL ADD-INS

  · *For a burst of freshness, sprinkle chopped parsley, basil, or cilantro over the grilled vegetables before serving.*

  · *To brighten the flavor, squeeze fresh lemon or lime juice over the vegetables just before serving.*

  · *For a smoky or spicy kick, add a pinch of smoked paprika, chili powder, or red pepper flakes to the oil mixture.*

CREAMY DILL EGG SALAD

SERVES: **4 (2 ½ CUPS)**

PREP TIME: **10 MINUTES**

COOK TIME: **12 MINUTES**

8 hard-boiled eggs, chopped

½ cup mayonnaise

2 tablespoons chopped fresh chives, plus extra for garnish

2 tablespoons chopped fresh dill, plus extra for garnish

2 teaspoons Dijon mustard

½ teaspoon garlic powder

¼ teaspoon smoked paprika

¼ teaspoon sea salt

¼ teaspoon black pepper

Put all of the ingredients in a large bowl and mix until well incorporated. Serve garnished with extra herbs.

TIPS & NOTES

- *This egg salad is delicious all on its own, or served on toast, wrapped in lettuce, or even as a sandwich.*

- **To hard-boil eggs:** *Place the eggs in a saucepan and cover with cold water by about an inch. Bring to a boil over medium-high heat. Cover the pot, remove from the heat, and let sit for 10 to 12 minutes. Transfer the eggs to an ice bath to cool for 5 minutes, then peel.*

- FLAVOR ADD-INS
  - *Celery or pickles for some crunch*
  - *Diced red onion for a sharp bite*
  - *Green olives or capers for a briny twist*
  - *Shredded cheddar and crumbled bacon for a loaded version*
  - *Diced avocado for creaminess and healthy fats*
  - *Greek yogurt (instead of mayo) for a protein boost*

BACON and GRUYÈRE EGG BITES

MAKES: **10 EGG BITES**

PREP TIME: **15 MINUTES**

COOK TIME: **15 MINUTES**

6 large eggs

1 cup cottage cheese

⅓ cup freshly grated Parmesan cheese

⅓ cup freshly shredded Gruyère cheese

3 tablespoons salted butter, melted

2 teaspoons white vinegar

2 teaspoons cornstarch

2 teaspoons tapioca starch

1 teaspoon hot sauce

½ teaspoon sea salt

½ cup finely chopped cooked bacon

SPECIAL EQUIPMENT:
Silicone egg bite mold with lid

1. Put the eggs, cottage cheese, half of the Parmesan, half of the Gruyère, the butter, vinegar, cornstarch, tapioca starch, hot sauce, and salt in a blender and pulse until smooth.

2. Place some of the bacon in the bottom of each well of a silicone egg bite mold. Top each with a little of the Parmesan and Gruyère. Gently press the cheese and bacon into the bottom of the mold. Pour in the egg mixture, filling the wells to just below the top.

3. Put the lid on the mold and place in a large pot (I use a 6-quart Dutch oven). Carefully fill the pan with water to right below the lid of the silicone mold. Bring the water to a rolling boil over high heat, then reduce the heat to medium, cover the pot, and steam for 12 to 15 minutes, until the egg bites are spongy in texture. They should have some spring to the touch but be not runny in the center.

4. Remove the mold from the water, uncover, and let the egg bites cool for 5 minutes before removing from the mold.

5. Repeat the process with remaining bacon, cheese, and egg mixture.

TIPS & NOTES

- *A standard-size silicone egg bite mold has 7 wells. This recipe makes 10 egg bites. You can double the recipe and get 20 egg bites if you fill each well to the top.*

- *For extra crispiness, I recommend popping the bites in the air fryer for a few minutes after taking them out of the mold. Air-fry at 350°F or 400°F for 5 to 6 minutes, until the outsides start to get golden brown and crispy. You can also broil them in your conventional oven—1 to 2 minutes should do the trick.*

BAKED HAM and EGG SKILLET

SERVES: **4**

PREP TIME: **10 MINUTES**

COOK TIME: **20 MINUTES**

2 tablespoons salted butter

⅔ cup chopped cooked ham steak

⅓ cup sliced leeks

½ cup heavy cream

¼ cup sour cream

2 tablespoons pesto

½ teaspoon sea salt

¼ cup shredded Gruyère cheese

8 large eggs

¼ cup crumbled goat cheese

Roughly torn fresh basil, for garnish

Cracked black pepper, for garnish

1. Preheat the oven to 400°F.

2. In a large ovenproof skillet, heat the butter over medium heat until melted and hot. Add the ham and leeks and cook until the leeks are softened and the ham has crisped up, about 8 minutes. Remove from the pan and set aside.

3. To the same skillet, add the cream, sour cream, pesto, and salt and whisk to combine. Bring to a slow boil over medium-low heat and then turn off the heat. Sprinkle with the Gruyère and most of the ham and leeks, reserving some for garnish.

4. Crack the eggs into individual ramekins, then gently slide each egg into the sauce. Transfer the skillet to the oven and bake until the egg whites are set and the yolks have reached the desired level of doneness. Top with the reserved ham and leeks, the goat cheese, basil, and cracked black pepper.

> **TIPS & NOTES**
>
> - *Leeks can trap dirt between their layers, so it's important to clean them thoroughly. Start by cutting off the dark green tops (you can save these for making stock) and trimming the root end. Slice the leek lengthwise, then fan the layers open under running water to rinse out any dirt or grit. You can also slice the leek into half-moons and soak the pieces in a bowl of water, gently agitating them to loosen the dirt before draining.*
>
> - *Swap out the ham steak for bacon, prosciutto, or even leftover Lemon-Herb Roasted Chicken (page 145). For a delicious vegetarian version, substitute the ham with sautéed mushrooms and spinach.*
>
> - *Pair with a nice crusty bread or toasted sourdough to scoop up the creamy sauce.*

124   SIMPLY**DELICIOUS**

FREEZER BREAKFAST SANDWICHES

SERVES: **12**

PREP TIME: **10 MINUTES**

COOK TIME: **20 MINUTES**

12 large eggs

1 cup cottage cheese

1 tablespoon Herby Everything Seasoning (page 314)

12 English muffins, toasted

4 cooked sausage patties (English muffin size)

4 slices American cheese

8 slices cooked bacon

4 slices white cheddar cheese

8 slices Canadian bacon or ham, warmed

4 slices Swiss cheese

SPECIAL EQUIPMENT:

Silicone muffin top pan

1. Preheat the oven to 300°F.

2. Put the eggs, cottage cheese, and seasoning in a blender and pulse until smooth. Divide the mixture evenly between 12 wells of a silicone muffin top pan. Bake for 15 minutes, or until the eggs are cooked through and soft with a spongy texture, but not browned. (While the eggs are cooking, toast the English muffins, cook the sausage and bacon, and warm the ham.) Let the eggs cool before removing from the mold.

3. You'll be making 12 egg sandwiches: 4 with sausage and American cheese, 4 with bacon and cheddar, and 4 with ham and Swiss. To assemble each sandwich, start with a bottom muffin, then layer the meat, cheese, egg, and top muffin.

4. Wrap each sandwich in parchment paper and then wrap again in foil. Use a permanent marker to label each sandwich with the type and date. Freeze for up to a month.

TIPS & NOTES

- *Mix and match any meats and cheeses you prefer. I also like to add sautéed peppers and onions, avocado, and fresh spinach or arugula.*

- *The sandwiches can be reheated in the microwave (without the foil), in the oven, or on the stovetop. But my favorite way to reheat them is in the microwave and air fryer—both! I take one out of the freezer and put it in the refrigerator the night before to thaw. When it's time to reheat, I remove the foil and microwave the sandwich in the parchment paper for 1 minute. Then I open it up, split it in half, and air-fry it until the English muffin starts to crisp up, the cheese is melted, and the sandwich is warmed through.*

ONE-POT
WONDERS

Of all the quick and easy cooking methods in this cookbook, one-pot dishes are perhaps my favorite because you aren't locked into any single cooking method. The possibilities are endless, with the only limitation being the number of pans you'll be dirtying—one! This makes for an easy cooking process, and an even easier cleanup.

WHAT MAKES ONE-POT COOKING SO GREAT?

Less cleanup: The most obvious perk...fewer dirty dishes! By cooking everything in one skillet, pot, sheet pan, or slow cooker, cleanup is a breeze. Simply put, less mess means more time to relax after dinner.

Flavor building: One-pot cooking allows flavors to truly come together. When a bunch of ingredients are cooked in the same vessel, their flavors meld and deepen, while spices and herbs infuse every element of the dish. For example, a quick splash of stock can deglaze a pan, allowing you to scrape up and mix in the delicious caramelized bits stuck to the bottom of the pan, "the fond" as it is called, where the flavor lives. Or browning the meat first, removing it, and returning it later helps to prevent overcooking while allowing flavors to develop as you continue to layer ingredients throughout the cooking process. All of this helps create richer, more complex flavors than you'd get from cooking ingredients separately.

Time saving: Many one-pot recipes come together in under an hour, and some in less than 30 minutes, making them a great option for busy weeknights. One-pot cooking is the perfect solution when time is limited but you still want something homemade.

Versatility: One-pot meals are incredibly forgiving, which makes them ideal for cooks who love to improvise. Have leftover vegetables? Toss them in! An extra can of beans or some leftover rice? Add them to the mix. The adaptability of one-pot meals means you can use what you have on hand, reducing food waste while creating unique and delicious dishes.

ONE-POT COOKING METHODS

One-pot dishes can be cooked using a variety of methods, each contributing its own take on flavor and texture. Here are some of the most common methods.

SAUTÉING AND STIR-FRYING

For quick, light one-pot meals, sautéing or stir-frying is the way to go. These methods are perfect for cooking everything from vegetables and grains to meat and seafood all in one pan. The keys to success are high heat and a hot pan, which allow the ingredients to sear quickly, locking in flavors and textures. The high heat also creates a perfect balance of crisp-tender vegetables and proteins that stay juicy.

SIMMERING

Simmering, which is at the heart of many one-pot meals, means cooking slowly in liquid over low heat to allow flavors to meld and ingredients to tenderize. When simmering, it's important to build layers of flavor by first sautéing aromatics, such as garlic, onions, and spices, then searing a protein to form a nice, caramelized crust, and finally adding liquid to simmer the ingredients to create a level of flavor that enhances the entire dish.

STEWING AND BRAISING

Cooking tougher cuts of meat in liquid over a longer period of time helps break down connective tissues, tenderizing the meat. Whether you're working with a whole chicken, beef chuck roast, or pork shoulder, the slow-cooked nature of stewing allows for deep flavor penetration and an irresistibly juicy texture.

ROASTING

With roasting, vegetables and proteins are typically cooked dry or with just a small amount of fat, allowing them to caramelize and develop deep roasted flavors.

SLOW COOKING

Slow cooking rewards patience. The slow cooker (aka crock pot) gently steams and tenderizes ingredients over a longer period, allowing the flavors to develop without requiring constant attention. This method works particularly well for soups, stews, curries, and braised dishes, all of which benefit from slow and steady heat.

SHEET PAN COOKING

Sheet pan meals are an efficient method for creating flavorful one-pot dishes with minimal hands-on time required. By arranging ingredients in a single layer on a rimmed baking sheet (referred to throughout as a sheet pan), you can achieve a perfectly balanced meal that combines protein, vegetables, and sometimes even grains, all cooked at once. The key to a successful sheet pan meal is choosing ingredients with similar cooking times, or placing denser ingredients, like root vegetables, on the pan first to allow them extra time to cook.

AIR FRYER COOKING

Air fryer meals have quickly become a favorite for those looking to prepare crispy, flavorful dishes without the hassle of deep frying or multiple cooking vessels. The air fryer uses hot air circulation to mimic the effect of frying, creating a crispy, golden exterior while keeping the inside moist and tender. While air fryers are often thought of for making appetizers or snacks like fries, the beauty of air fryer meals is their speed. Ingredients cook much faster than they would in a conventional oven, thanks to the intense, direct heat in a much smaller space.

THE ART OF LAYERING FLAVORS

This exact formula doesn't work for every cooking method I mentioned above, but it works well for simmering, stewing, braising, sautéing, and even slow cooking—if you are willing to put in the extra time and effort.

1. **Start with aromatics:** Sauté onions, garlic, shallots, ginger, or other aromatics in a bit of oil or butter until soft and fragrant.

2. **Brown your protein:** For meat-based dishes, sear chicken, beef, or pork in olive oil or butter until golden brown with a nice, caramelized crust. This step locks in juices.

3. **Toast spices:** Toast spices in oil for a few seconds to release their aromas. Be careful not to burn.

4. **Deglaze the pot:** Use wine, stock, or even water to deglaze the pot and then scrape up and mix in any browned bits stuck to the bottom of the pan. This step intensifies the flavor.

5. **Simmer and combine:** Add grains, pasta, or vegetables, plus liquids like stock, wine, or cream. Let everything simmer gently until finished cooking.

6. **Finish strong:** Depending on the type of meal, a squeeze of lemon, a swirl of cream, a handful of fresh herbs, or a sprinkle of cheese, can take your dish to the next level.

The beauty of one-pot cooking lies in its balance of efficiency and versatility. One-pot recipes are proof that mouthwatering dishes don't require complicated techniques and endless cleanup. Using a handful of everyday ingredients and a single cooking vessel, you can create meals that are deeply satisfying and bursting with flavor.

JAMBALAYA

SERVES: **4**

PREP TIME: **25 MINUTES**

COOK TIME: **35 MINUTES**

1 tablespoon olive oil

1 pound andouille sausage, cut into ¼-inch-thick slices

1½ pounds boneless, skinless chicken thighs, cut into bite-size pieces

3 tablespoons salted butter

3 tablespoons all-purpose flour

1 medium yellow onion, chopped

4 green onions, sliced, green and white parts separated

4 cloves garlic, minced

3 ribs celery, chopped

1 green bell pepper, seeded and chopped

1 (14.5-ounce) can diced tomatoes, with juices

1 tablespoon Cajun seasoning

2 teaspoons dried basil

1 teaspoon sea salt

½ teaspoon black pepper

¼ teaspoon cayenne pepper (optional)

2½ cups chicken stock

1¼ cups long-grain white rice

1 pound medium raw shrimp, peeled and tails removed

1. Heat the olive oil in a large high-sided skillet or Dutch oven over medium-high heat. Add the sausage and chicken and sear until browned on all sides. The chicken may not be fully cooked at this stage. Transfer the meats to a bowl.

2. Reduce the heat to medium and add the butter and flour to the pan. Stir, scraping up and mixing in any bits that are stuck to the bottom of the pan. Add the yellow onion, the white parts of the green onions, the garlic, celery, and bell pepper and sauté for 3 minutes. Add the diced tomatoes, Cajun seasoning, basil, salt, black pepper, and cayenne, if using, and mix until the ingredients are well combined.

3. Stir in the stock and rice. Bring to a gentle boil, then return the chicken and sausage to the pan. Reduce the heat to a simmer, cover, and cook for 15 minutes.

4. Mix in the shrimp, cover, and cook for an additional 5 minutes, or until the rice is tender. Garnish with the green parts of the green onions before serving.

TIPS & NOTES

- *If you can't find andouille sausage, try smoked sausage, chorizo, or even kielbasa for a different depth of flavor.*

- *If the jambalaya looks too dry while simmering, add a little more stock, a splash at a time. If it's too soupy, let it simmer uncovered for a few extra minutes.*

- *Try substituting duck, crab, or even leftover roasted turkey for a unique twist.*

BEEF BIRRIA

SERVES: **6**

PREP TIME: **20 MINUTES**

COOK TIME: **2½ HOURS**

2 tablespoons olive oil

5 pounds chuck roast, cut into 2- to 3-inch chunks

Sea salt

2 teaspoons dried Mexican oregano

2 bay leaves

1 teaspoon chili powder

1 teaspoon ground cumin

½ teaspoon ground cloves

6 cloves garlic, peeled

1 large onion, peeled and sliced in half with the stem left on

8 cups beef stock

3 dried guajillo chiles, stemmed and seeded

3 dried chiles de arbol, stemmed and seeded

FOR SERVING

Chopped red onion

Chopped fresh cilantro

Lime wedges

1. Heat the olive oil in a large stockpot or Dutch oven over medium heat. Season the chuck roast pieces generously with salt on all sides. Add the pieces to the pot and cook until browned, about 10 minutes.

2. Add the oregano, bay leaves, chili powder, cumin, and cloves to the pot and stir to coat the beef in the spices. Add the garlic cloves and onion halves, then pour in the stock. Increase the heat to high and bring to a boil. Skim the foam from the top and discard. Add the dried chiles, lower the heat, and simmer for 10 minutes.

3. Remove the chiles and garlic cloves from the broth and transfer to a high-powered blender or food processor. Add three or four ladles of the broth to the blender and blend until smooth.

4. Through a fine-mesh sieve, strain the blended chiles back into the soup. Reduce the heat to low and simmer for 2 to 3 hours, stirring every 30 to 45 minutes, until the meat is tender.

5. Taste and add more salt, if desired. Skim any grease from the broth and discard (or use to make Quesabirria Tacos, page 321). Remove the onion halves and serve the birria with red onion, cilantro, and a squeeze of lime.

> **TIPS & NOTES**
>
> - *Beef birria is a rich, slow-cooked Mexican stew made with tender braised beef in a deeply flavorful, smoky, and slightly spicy consommé. Traditionally from Jalisco, birria was originally made with goat, but beef (birria de res) has become widely popular.*
>
> - *In addition to chuck roast, you can make it with oxtail, beef short ribs, brisket, beef shank, lamb, goat, or a combination of any of these.*
>
> - *I used dried guajillo chiles and chiles de arbol, but you can also use pasilla, ancho, or Morita chiles.*

PORK CHOPS with LEMON-THYME PAN SAUCE

SERVES: **4**

PREP TIME: **10 MINUTES**

COOK TIME: **25 MINUTES**

4 (8-ounce) bone-in pork chops (about 2 pounds)

Sea salt and black pepper

2 tablespoons olive oil

1 shallot, finely chopped

¼ cup cooking sherry

1 cup chicken stock

2 fresh thyme sprigs

1 lemon, sliced into wheels

2 tablespoons salted butter

1. Season the pork chops generously on both sides with salt and pepper. Heat the olive oil in a large skillet over medium-high heat. Add the chops and sear on both sides until golden brown and a slight crust has formed. Remove the pork chops from the pan, cover, and set aside.

2. Reduce the heat to medium, add the shallots to the pan, and cook for 2 to 3 minutes, until slightly softened. Add the sherry and deglaze, scraping up and mixing in any bits stuck to the bottom of the pan. Add the stock, thyme sprigs, and lemon slices and bring to a boil. Reduce the heat to low and simmer until the sauce has reduced by half. Add the butter and swirl it with a spatula to melt it into the sauce.

3. Return the pork chops to the pan and cook until they are cooked through (see note below about cooking temperatures). I recommend using a meat thermometer: Pork is fully cooked once it has reached an internal temperature of 145°F, but you can cook it further per personal preference. Serve the chops drizzled with the pan sauce.

TIPS & NOTES

- *I love to serve these with my Garlic-Herb Mashed Potatoes (page 189) and Umami Brussels Sprouts (page 259).*

- **145°F – Medium-Rare to Medium:** *Slightly pink, juicy, and tender.*

- **150 to 155°F – Medium-Well:** *Less pink, firmer texture.*

- **160°F+ – Well-Done:** *Fully cooked, drier texture.*

CABBAGE ROLL in a BOWL

SERVES: **4**

PREP TIME: **15 MINUTES**

COOK TIME: **35 MINUTES**

2 tablespoons salted butter

2 tablespoons olive oil

1 medium sweet onion, diced

3 cloves garlic, minced

1½ pounds ground beef

8 ounces ground pork

¾ cup beef stock

2 teaspoons dried oregano

2 teaspoons sea salt

1 teaspoon black pepper

1 teaspoon paprika

1 teaspoon garlic powder

1 teaspoon onion powder

½ teaspoon dried thyme

2 (15-ounce) cans diced tomatoes, drained

1 (6-ounce) can tomato paste

2 tablespoons balsamic vinegar

1 medium head green cabbage, halved and sliced

2 cups cooked long-grain rice

2 tablespoons chopped fresh flat-leaf parsley, for garnish

1. Heat the butter and olive oil in a large skillet or Dutch oven over medium heat. Add the onion and garlic and cook until the onion is translucent and the garlic is fragrant, about 8 minutes.

2. Add the ground beef and pork and, using a wooden spatula to break up the meat, cook until browned, about 8 minutes. Drain any excess grease.

3. Add the stock, oregano, salt, pepper, paprika, garlic powder, onion powder, and thyme. Bring to a boil, then reduce the heat to low and simmer for 5 minutes.

4. Add the diced tomatoes, tomato paste, balsamic vinegar, cabbage, and rice. Increase the heat to medium-low and cook for 20 minutes, or until the cabbage is wilted and tender. Taste and add more salt, if desired. Garnish with the parsley before serving.

TIPS & NOTES

- *Add a few extra cups of beef stock to create a hearty cabbage roll soup.*

- *Slow Cooker Option: Brown the meat and sauté the onion and garlic first, then transfer everything to a slow cooker and cook on low for 6 to 8 hours.*

- *Use ground turkey or chicken instead of beef and pork for a leaner, higher protein version.*

LEMON-HERB ROASTED CHICKEN

6 tablespoons salted butter, softened

2 teaspoons grated lemon zest

2 teaspoons dried thyme

2 teaspoons rubbed sage

2 teaspoons dried minced onion

1 teaspoon garlic powder

1 teaspoon sea salt

½ teaspoon black pepper

1 (4-pound) whole chicken

1½ cups chicken stock

Juice of 1 lemon

1 lemon, cut into wheels

1 medium onion, peeled and cut into large chunks

2 fresh rosemary sprigs

1. Preheat the oven to 400°F.

2. Put the butter, lemon zest, thyme, sage, dried onion, garlic powder, salt, and pepper in a small bowl and mix until the ingredients are well incorporated.

3. Place the chicken, breast side up, in a shallow roasting pan with a rack in it. Add the stock, lemon juice, lemon wheels, onion chunks, and rosemary sprigs to the bottom of the pan. Gently loosen the skin covering the breast of the chicken, lifting it away from the breast and creating a pocket between the breast and the skin. Pack half of the herbed butter into the pocket, distributing it evenly. Rub the other half of the herbed butter all over the top of the chicken.

4. Roast on the middle rack for 30 minutes. Take the chicken out of the oven, baste with the juices, and return it to the oven. Roast for an additional 30 to 45 minutes, basting every 10 minutes, until it is cooked all the way through (a meat thermometer inserted into the thickest part of the breast registers 165°F) and the skin is nice and crispy.

TIPS & NOTES

- *Similar to the Herbed Butter Spatchcocked Chicken (page 64), you can add root vegetables like carrots, parsnips, potatoes, or sweet potatoes to the roasting pan. They'll soak up the chicken juices for extra flavor.*

- *Always use a meat thermometer to ensure chicken is cooked to 165°F. Insert it into the thickest part of the breast without touching the bone.*

- *Dry the chicken thoroughly with paper towels before seasoning—it's key for crispy skin!*

- *Baste the chicken regularly in the second half of cooking to keep it juicy and prevent the skin from drying out. Use a spoon or turkey baster to pour the pan juices over the chicken.*

FRENCH ONION CHICKEN

4 (6-ounce) boneless, skinless chicken breasts (about 1½ pounds)

Sea salt and black pepper

4 tablespoons salted butter, divided

2 medium yellow onions, thinly sliced

3 cloves garlic, minced

1 cup beef stock

½ cup cooking sherry

1 tablespoon Worcestershire sauce

1 tablespoon fresh thyme leaves, plus extra for garnish

1 cup shredded mozzarella cheese

½ cup shredded Gruyère cheese

1. Lightly season the chicken breasts on both sides with salt and pepper.

2. In a large ovenproof skillet over medium-low heat, combine 2 tablespoons of the butter, the onions, and garlic. Cook, stirring occasionally, until the onions are nice and caramelized, about 30 minutes. Remove the onions from the pan and set aside.

3. Add the remaining 2 tablespoons of butter to the skillet and melt over medium-high heat. Add the chicken breasts and sear on both sides until they are a deep golden brown, 8 to 10 minutes. (They will not be fully cooked at this stage.) Remove the chicken from the pan and set aside.

4. Deglaze the pan with the stock, using a rubber spatula to scrape up and mix in any remaining bits of chicken stuck to the bottom. Simmer for 3 to 5 minutes. Reduce the heat to medium-low and add the sherry, Worcestershire, thyme, 1 teaspoon of salt, and ½ teaspoon of pepper. Simmer until the sauce has reduced by half and thickened slightly, about 6 minutes.

5. Preheat the oven to 275°F.

6. Return the caramelized onions to the pan and nestle in the chicken. Simmer until the chicken is cooked all the way through and has reached an internal temperature of 165°F, about 10 minutes.

7. Spoon the onions and some sauce over the chicken, then top with the Gruyère and mozzarella cheeses. Transfer to the oven and bake for 7 to 8 minutes, until the cheese is melted and bubbly. Spoon a little bit of onion gravy on top of each piece of chicken, garnish with fresh thyme, and serve.

TIPS & NOTES

- *If you don't have cooking sherry, dry white wine or extra beef stock works as a substitute.*

- *Stir in a splash of heavy cream at the end for a richer sauce.*

- *Use boneless, skinless chicken thighs for a juicier option, or swap in pork chops or even steak for a different protein.*

- *Instead of Gruyère, try Swiss, provolone, or white cheddar for a similar melt and flavor.*

CREAMY CHICKEN MARSALA

SERVES: **4**

PREP TIME: **15 MINUTES**

COOK TIME: **30 MINUTES**

4 (6-ounce) boneless, skinless chicken breasts (about 1½ pounds)

¼ cup all-purpose flour

Sea salt and black pepper

1 tablespoon olive oil

3 tablespoons salted butter, divided

10 ounces cremini mushrooms, sliced

1 medium shallot, finely chopped

3 cloves garlic, minced

⅓ cup chicken stock

¾ cup dry Marsala wine

⅔ cup heavy cream

2 teaspoons chopped fresh thyme

2 tablespoons chopped fresh flat-leaf parsley, for garnish

1. Pound the chicken breasts until they are ¼ to ½ inch thick. Then cut each piece in half to make 8 cutlets.

2. Whisk together the flour, 1 teaspoon of salt, and ½ teaspoon of pepper in a large shallow bowl until well combined. Dredge the chicken in the flour mixture, coating both sides evenly and generously.

3. Heat the olive oil and 2 tablespoons of the butter in a large skillet over medium-high heat. Add the chicken and cook, flipping only once, until the pieces are golden brown on both sides, about 5 minutes per side. It may not be fully cooked through at this stage. Transfer the chicken to a plate and cover.

4. Add the remaining tablespoon of butter to the pan. Add the mushrooms and cook until they have released their liquid and started to brown, 3 to 4 minutes. Add the shallot and garlic and cook until tender and fragrant, 1 to 2 minutes. Pour in a splash of the stock to deglaze the pan, scraping up and mixing in any browned bits that are stuck to the bottom. Add the remaining stock, the Marsala, cream, thyme, ¾ teaspoon of salt, and ½ teaspoon of pepper. Bring to a boil, then reduce the heat to medium-low and simmer, uncovered, until the sauce has reduced by almost half and thickened, 10 to 12 minutes.

5. Return the chicken to the pan, along with any juices on the plate. Reduce the heat to low and simmer until the chicken is warmed through and fully cooked. Taste and add more salt and pepper, if desired. Garnish with the parsley and serve.

TIPS & NOTES

- *To save time and prep work, buy chicken cutlets instead of pounding out chicken breasts.*

- *Or swap out the chicken breasts for boneless thighs for an even juicier option, or use thinly sliced pork chops or veal cutlets for a twist on the classic.*

CHICKEN SCALLOPINI with TOMATOES

SERVES: **4**

PREP TIME: **15 MINUTES**

COOK TIME: **20 MINUTES**

1½ pounds chicken cutlets or thinly sliced chicken breasts

Sea salt and black pepper

1 tablespoon olive oil

3 tablespoons salted butter

2 tablespoons capers, drained

1 cup chicken stock

2 tablespoons fresh lemon juice

20 grape or cherry tomatoes (mix of colors)

2 tablespoons chopped fresh flat-leaf parsley, for garnish

1. Season the chicken generously on both sides with salt and pepper. Heat the olive oil in a large skillet over medium-high heat. Add the chicken and cook until browned on both sides and cooked through, 2 to 3 minutes per side. Remove from the pan and cover to keep warm.

2. Reduce the heat to medium and add the butter and capers to the skillet. Cook until the capers are hot and sizzling, about 3 minutes. Pour in the stock and lemon juice and deglaze the pan, using a rubber spatula to scrape up and mix in any bits that are stuck to the bottom.

3. Increase the heat to medium-high and bring to a boil. Simmer until the sauce has reduced by one-third, about 5 minutes. Lower the heat to medium and add the tomatoes. Cook until soft and slightly blistered, about 3 minutes.

4. Return the chicken to the pan and spoon the sauce over the top. Garnish with the parsley and serve.

TIPS & NOTES

- *This recipe is also delicious with pork or veal cutlets.*

- *If you don't have capers, substitute chopped green olives for a nice briny punch.*

- *I love to serve the chicken and sauce over angel hair pasta, risotto, or Garlic-Herb Mashed Potatoes (page 189).*

CREAMY GARLIC SCALLOPS PICCATA

SERVES: **4**

PREP TIME: **10 MINUTES**

COOK TIME: **15 MINUTES**

1¼ pounds sea scallops

Sea salt and black pepper

2 tablespoons olive oil

2 tablespoons salted butter

5 cloves garlic, minced

⅓ cup dry white wine or chicken stock

1 cup heavy cream

1 teaspoon grated lemon zest

1 tablespoon fresh lemon juice

¼ cup capers, drained

2 tablespoons chopped fresh flat-leaf parsley, for garnish

Lemon slices, for serving

1. If needed, remove the side muscle from each scallop. Thoroughly pat the scallops dry with paper towels. (The drier they are, the better they will sear.) Season generously on both sides with salt and pepper.

2. Heat the olive oil in a large skillet over medium-high heat until starting to sizzle. Add the scallops in a single layer, being sure not to crowd the pan, which would cause them to steam rather than sear. You may need to sear them in batches to give them the proper space in the pan. Sear the scallops for 2 minutes on each side, or until a nice golden brown crust forms. Transfer the scallops to a plate and cover.

3. Lower the heat to medium, add the butter and garlic to the pan, and cook until the garlic is fragrant, about 1 minute. Deglaze the pan with the wine, scraping up and mixing in any browned bits that are stuck to the bottom. Simmer for 2 to 3 minutes, until the wine has reduced by about half.

4. Add the cream, lemon zest, and lemon juice and bring to a boil. Turn down the heat to medium-low and simmer until the sauce has reduced by about half and thickened, 6 to 8 minutes. Stir in the capers.

5. Return the scallops and any juices on the plate to the pan and cook until warmed through. Garnish with parsley and serve with lemon slices.

TIPS & NOTES

- *Dry white wine adds depth and acidity, but chicken stock works as a flavorful nonalcoholic alternative. A splash of apple cider vinegar or white wine vinegar can mimic the tang of wine.*

- *For a dairy-free version, use coconut cream or cashew cream instead of heavy cream, and replace the butter with dairy-free butter or olive oil.*

- *Try shrimp, lobster, or even chicken cutlets if scallops aren't available. Cooking times may vary slightly.*

PESTO STEAMED CLAMS

2 pounds Manila clams (or other small clams)

1 teaspoon salt

½ cup (1 stick) salted butter

4 cloves garlic, minced

1 cup clam juice

¾ cup pesto

1 small lemon, cut into wedges, for serving

1. Soak the clams for 20 minutes in a large bowl of water mixed with the salt. This will help purge any sand from the clams. Drain and, if any clams are open, give them a tap. If they close, they are still fresh, but if they remain open, they should be discarded.

2. Melt the butter in a large sauté pan over medium heat. Add the garlic and cook until fragrant, about 30 seconds. Add the clam juice and pesto, increase the heat to high, and bring to a boil.

3. Add the clams and reduce the heat to medium. Cover and steam, shaking the pan occasionally, until all of the clams have opened, 6 to 8 minutes. (You can shake the pan, but do not stir, as the clams may come out of their shells and fall into the broth.) Serve with lemon wedges.

TIPS & NOTES

- *This recipe can be made using cockles or mussels as well.*

- *I love to serve the clams with a nice crusty bread to soak up all of the pesto broth.*

PHILLY CHEESESTEAK FRENCH ONION SOUP

SERVES: **4**

PREP TIME: **15 MINUTES**

COOK TIME: **55 MINUTES**

4 tablespoons olive oil, divided

3 large yellow onions, thinly sliced

2 tablespoons salted butter

1 tablespoon Worcestershire sauce

4 cloves garlic, minced

1 tablespoon fresh thyme leaves, or 1 teaspoon dried thyme, plus extra for garnish

2 bay leaves

Sea salt and black pepper

½ cup cooking sherry

4 cups beef stock

2 small bell peppers (red, green, and/or yellow), seeded and thinly sliced

1 (10-ounce) rib-eye steak, thinly sliced

8 small slices French bread or baguette, toasted

4 slices provolone cheese

1¼ cups shredded Gruyère cheese

1. Heat 3 tablespoons of the olive oil in a large Dutch oven or stockpot over medium heat. Add the onions and sauté until soft, about 12 minutes. Add the butter and continue cooking until the onions start to brown, about 10 minutes. Stir in the Worcestershire sauce, garlic, thyme, bay leaves, ½ teaspoon of salt, and ½ teaspoon of black pepper and cook for 5 minutes.

2. Deglaze the pan with the sherry, using a rubber spatula to scrape up and mix in any bits that are stuck to the bottom. Add the stock, bring to a boil, and reduce the heat to low. Simmer for 25 minutes.

3. While the broth is simmering, heat the remaining tablespoon of oil in a large skillet over medium heat. Add the bell peppers, sprinkle with a little salt and black pepper, and sauté for 5 minutes. Add the steak and cook until it reaches the desired doneness. Transfer the cooked peppers and steak to the soup. Taste and add more salt, if desired.

4. Preheat the oven to broil.

5. Discard the bay leaves and divide the soup evenly among four large ovenproof ramekins. Top each with two pieces of toasted bread and a slice of provolone. Divide the Gruyère evenly among the ramekins. Place the ramekins under the broiler and cook until the cheese is bubbly and browned. Garnish with fresh thyme and a sprinkle of black pepper before serving.

TIPS & NOTES

- *Rib eye adds incredible richness, but you can use sirloin, shaved beef, or even leftover roast beef for a budget-friendly option.*

- *Caramelizing the onions properly is crucial—don't rush this step! The longer they cook, the sweeter and richer the soup will be. Aim for a deep golden-brown color.*

- *Keep a close eye on the soup while broiling—cheese can go from perfectly golden to burnt in seconds! Move the ramekins closer or farther from the broiler to control browning.*

ROASTED RED PEPPER, TOMATO, and SMOKED GOUDA BISQUE

SERVES: **8**

PREP TIME: **15 MINUTES**

COOK TIME: **50 MINUTES**

3 tablespoons salted butter

1 medium yellow onion, diced

3 large cloves garlic, minced

2 tablespoons tomato paste

2 teaspoons dried basil

1½ teaspoons sea salt

1 teaspoon dried oregano

½ teaspoon black pepper

3 cups chicken stock, divided

2 (14.5-ounce) cans fire-roasted tomatoes, with juices

1 (12-ounce) jar roasted red peppers, with juices

½ cup heavy cream

8 ounces smoked Gouda cheese, shredded

Croutons, for serving

Fresh basil leaves, for garnish

1. Heat the butter in a large Dutch oven or stockpot over medium heat. Add the onions and garlic and sauté until the onions are translucent and the garlic is fragrant, about 8 minutes. Add the tomato paste, basil, salt, oregano, and pepper and sauté for 5 minutes.

2. Deglaze the pot with ½ cup of the stock, using a rubber spatula to scrape up and mix in any bits that are stuck to the bottom. Add the fire-roasted tomatoes, roasted red peppers, and remaining 1½ cups of stock. Bring to a boil over high heat, then reduce the heat to low and simmer for 30 minutes. (The longer you let it simmer, the more the flavors will come together.)

3. Use an immersion blender to puree the soup to a smooth, silky consistency. Mix in the cream and Gouda and simmer for 15 minutes. Taste and add more salt and pepper, if desired. Top with croutons and fresh basil before serving.

TIPS & NOTES

- *Stir in shredded rotisserie chicken, crispy bacon, or cooked Italian sausage for a heartier bisque.*

- *Add ½ teaspoon of red pepper flakes or a dash of cayenne pepper to add a little kick.*

- *To make the soup vegetarian, swap out the chicken stock for vegetable stock.*

- *The bisque also makes an excellent pasta sauce.*

DILL PICKLE SOUP

4 tablespoons salted butter, divided

1 tablespoon olive oil

3 medium carrots, peeled and diced

3 ribs celery, diced

1 small yellow onion, diced

4 cloves garlic, minced

2 tablespoons all-purpose flour

1 teaspoon dried dill

1 teaspoon dried oregano

1 teaspoon dried thyme

1 teaspoon sea salt

½ teaspoon black pepper

½ teaspoon paprika

6 cups chicken stock

⅓ cup pickle juice, or more to taste

3 large russet potatoes, peeled and cut into 1-inch pieces (about 4 cups)

1 cup sour cream, room temperature

1 cup heavy cream

1 cup diced dill pickles

Sliced green onions, for garnish

1. Heat 2 tablespoons of the butter and the olive oil in a large Dutch oven or stockpot over medium heat. Add the carrots, celery, and onion and cook until the vegetables are tender, about 7 minutes. Remove the vegetables from the pot and set aside.

2. Melt the remaining 2 tablespoons of butter in the pot. Add the garlic and cook until fragrant, about 1 minute. Stir in the flour, dill, oregano, thyme, salt, pepper, and paprika and cook until lightly browned, 2 to 3 minutes.

3. Add the stock and pickle juice and stir until the ingredients are well combined. Bring to a boil over high heat and stir in the potatoes. Cook for 8 to 10 minutes, until the potatoes are soft. Reduce the heat to medium-low. Using an immersion blender, puree the soup right in the pot. It should be mostly creamy but with some visible chunks of potato.

4. Stir in the sour cream and heavy cream until well incorporated and smooth. Return the sautéed vegetables to the pot and add the pickles. Taste and add more pickle juice, if desired. Let simmer for an additional 15 minutes. Garnish with green onions before serving.

TIPS & NOTES

- *To make this soup low-carb, simply omit the flour and substitute cauliflower florets for the potatoes. This will bring it down to 8 grams of total carbohydrates per serving.*

- *To make it gluten-free, omit the flour and add a touch more heavy cream to help thicken the soup.*

- *For a vegetarian version, simply swap out the chicken stock for vegetable stock.*

- *For a vegan version, swap out the chicken stock for vegetable stock and the heavy cream and sour cream for your favorite nondairy alternatives.*

STEAMED ARTICHOKES

4 cups chicken stock

4 large artichokes

2 tablespoons dried minced onion

1½ teaspoons sea salt

2 bay leaves

Lemon-Caper Aioli (page 301), for serving

1. Bring the stock to a simmer in a large Dutch oven or stockpot over medium-high heat.

2. Cut away ½ to 1 inch from the top of each artichoke. Remove any dead or brown outer leaves. Cut off the stem close to the base so that the artichoke will stand upright.

3. Place the trimmed artichokes in the simmering broth, sprinkle with the dried onion and salt, and toss in the bay leaves. Cover and simmer for 45 minutes to 1 hour, until the artichokes are tender and the leaves are easily plucked. Serve with aioli for dipping.

TIPS & NOTES

- *To eat a steamed artichoke, start by plucking off the outer leaves one at a time. Dip the meaty base of a leaf into your sauce, then slide the leaf through closed teeth to scrape the tender flesh off the leaf (and discard the leaf). As you work your way inward, the leaves become softer and more tender. Once you've removed all of the leaves, you'll reach the fuzzy center, known as the choke. Scrape this inedible fuzzy part away with a spoon to reveal the artichoke heart—the most tender and flavorful part.*

- *These are also delicious with plain mayonnaise or melted salted butter.*

DUTCH OVEN RANCH POPCORN

SERVES: **4**

PREP TIME: **10 MINUTES**

COOK TIME: **10 MINUTES**

½ cup nutritional yeast, or more to taste

2 tablespoons dry ranch powder, or more to taste

1 teaspoon sea salt, or more to taste

2 tablespoons avocado oil

⅓ cup popcorn kernels

½ cup butter-flavored coconut oil, melted

1. In a small bowl, combine the nutritional yeast, ranch powder, and salt. Set aside.

2. Put the avocado oil and popcorn kernels in a Dutch oven, turn the heat to medium-high, and cover. Once you hear the kernels starting to pop, reduce the heat to medium. Once the popping starts to slow down, remove the pan from the heat and let the corn finish popping off the heat.

3. Toss the popcorn with the coconut oil and the desired amount of the seasoning mixture.

TIPS & NOTES

- *I like to make this recipe with butter-flavored coconut oil because it gives the popcorn more of a movie theater popcorn taste. But you can also use butter or ghee.*

- FLAVOR VARIATIONS

  · **Pumpkin Spice Popcorn:** *Instead of the seasonings listed, toss the popcorn with melted butter, pumpkin pie spice, and a bit of brown sugar.*

  · **Peanut Butter Cup Popcorn:** *Mix melted peanut butter and chocolate and drizzle over the popcorn. Add a pinch of sea salt for balance.*

  · **S'Mores Popcorn:** *Toss the popcorn with mini marshmallows, chocolate chips, and crushed graham crackers. Drizzle with melted chocolate.*

  · **Salt and Vinegar Popcorn:** *Toss the popcorn with melted butter, salt, and apple cider vinegar powder.*

  · **Rosemary Popcorn:** *Toss the popcorn with olive oil, freshly chopped rosemary, and flaky sea salt.*

  · **Truffle Parmesan Popcorn:** *Drizzle the popcorn with truffle oil and sprinkle with Parmesan and cracked black pepper.*

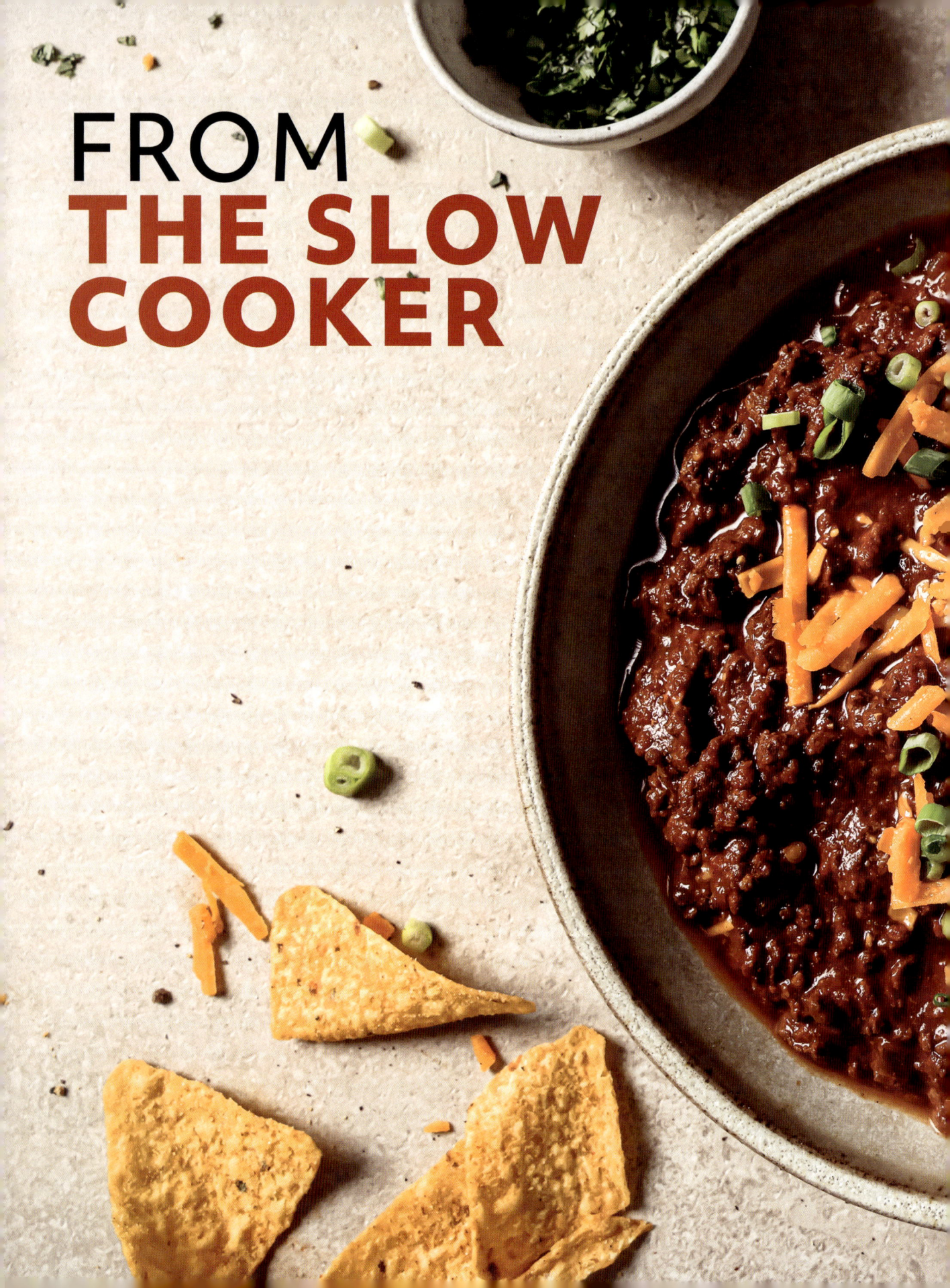

FROM
THE SLOW
COOKER

The slow cooker is a beloved kitchen tool that has transformed the way we approach cooking, making it easier and more efficient. With its humble yet versatile design, the slow cooker is an essential appliance that takes the stress out of preparing meals, allowing flavors to develop and deepen over hours without requiring constant attention.

Whether you're a busy professional, juggling multiple tasks, or simply looking to maximize convenience without sacrificing flavor, the slow cooker is the kitchen appliance for you. This chapter will show you how to harness its full potential.

THE BASICS OF SLOW COOKING

Slow cooking involves cooking food at a low temperature for an extended period of time and is *not* about rushing or forcing the food to cook quickly. The results are tender, juicy, and often fall-apart flavorful because slow cooking allows flavors to deepen over time. Slow cookers are built for ease of use, and most have a simple dial to set the temperature to Low, High, or Keep Warm. On the high setting, most dishes typically take 3 to 4 hours to cook, while the low setting allows for a longer cooking time of 6 to 8 hours or more. Both settings are designed to cook food slowly and evenly, and choosing the right setting depends largely on the recipe and how much time you have.

THE BEST INGREDIENTS FOR SLOW COOKING

This is not an exhaustive list, but rather some ideas to get you started.

PROTEIN

- **Beef:** Chuck roast, short ribs, brisket
- **Pork:** Shoulder, butt, ribs
- **Chicken:** Thighs, breasts, drumsticks, whole chicken
- **Lamb:** Shanks or shoulder
- **Legumes:** Dried beans and lentils

VEGETABLES

- **Root vegetables:** Potatoes, carrots, parsnips, beets
- **Squash:** Butternut, acorn, pumpkin
- **Sturdy greens:** Kale, collards, cabbage

FLAVOR ENHANCERS

- **Herbs:** Thyme, rosemary, bay leaves

- **Aromatics:** Onion, garlic, ginger

- **Spices:** Cumin, smoked paprika, chili powder

- **Sauces:** Soy sauce, fish sauce, coconut aminos, Worcestershire

- **Stock and broth:** Beef, chicken, vegetable

SLOW COOKING TIPS AND TRICKS

Although slow cooking is meant to be a laid-back process, a little extra effort up front can make a big difference in the final result. Here are some tips to help you cook more efficiently, avoid common pitfalls, and get the most out of your slow cooker.

USE THE RIGHT CUTS OF MEAT

Because slow cooking relies on low heat and long cooking times, tough cuts of meat are often the best choice. Cuts like chuck roast, pork shoulder, and chicken thighs contain more connective tissue and fat, which break down during the slow cooking process, making them tender and flavorful.

BROWN MEAT BEFOREHAND

While it's not strictly necessary to brown meat before adding it to the slow cooker, doing so really enhances the flavor. It's quick and easy to season meats generously with salt and pepper and then sear them in oil in a ripping hot pan before adding them to the slow cooker. The slow cooking after the sear then helps develop deeper flavor. It's a step that's worth the extra time, as it can elevate even the simplest recipes.

LAYER INGREDIENTS PROPERLY

One of the key elements of successful slow cooking is layering ingredients. Denser ingredients, such as root vegetables (especially potatoes), should be placed at the bottom of the slow cooker, where they will be in direct contact with the heat. More delicate items, like fresh herbs and dairy, should be added later in the cooking process. This ensures that the slower-cooking ingredients have ample time to cook and become tender without overcooking the more fragile ones.

DON'T OVERFILL THE SLOW COOKER

Slow cookers work best when they are filled about half to three-quarters full. Overfilling can prevent the heat from circulating properly, leading to uneven cooking. On the other hand, underfilling the slow cooker can result in faster evaporation of liquids, resulting in drier dishes. My go-to is a 7-quart slow cooker.

ADJUST COOKING TIMES FOR SMALLER OR LARGER QUANTITIES

If you're cooking a smaller or larger batch than a recipe calls for, you may need to adjust the cooking time. For smaller quantities, reduce the time by 25 to 30 percent. For larger quantities, you may need to add time. Keep in mind that slow cooking is a forgiving process, so slight adjustments won't drastically affect the outcome.

KEEP THE LID ON

One of the most tempting instincts when using a slow cooker is to lift the lid to check on the food as it cooks. While this might seem harmless, every time you open the lid you lose valuable heat and moisture, which can extend the cooking time and compromise the texture of the dish. Trust that your slow cooker is doing its job and resist the urge to peek.

There's something magical about walking into your home and being greeted by the aroma of a meal that's been cooking all day. Whether you're simmering a sauce, creating a hearty stew, or perfecting tender pulled pork, slow cooking offers more than just convenience—it offers flavor! So, plug in that slow cooker or dust off your Dutch oven. Let's celebrate patience, flavor, and the joy of hands-off cooking.

BALSAMIC SHORT RIBS

SERVES: **4**

PREP TIME: **15 MINUTES**

COOK TIME: **4 TO 8 HOURS**

8 bone-in beef short ribs (about 4 pounds)

1½ teaspoons sea salt

1 teaspoon black pepper

4 tablespoons olive oil, divided

3 large shallots, sliced

¼ cup tomato paste

4 cloves garlic, chopped

1½ teaspoons chopped fresh thyme

1¼ cups balsamic vinegar

¾ cup beef stock

2 sprigs fresh rosemary

3 tablespoons cornstarch

⅓ cup cold water

1 tablespoon chopped fresh flat-leaf parsley, for garnish

1. Season the ribs with the salt and pepper. Heat 2 tablespoons of the olive oil in a large skillet over medium-high heat. Add the ribs and cook until browned on all sides, about 6 minutes. Transfer the ribs to the slow cooker.

2. Add the remaining 2 tablespoons of olive oil and the shallots to the skillet. Cook, stirring occasionally, until the shallots start to brown, 3 to 5 minutes. Stir in the tomato paste, garlic, and thyme and cook until the shallots are evenly coated, about 2 minutes. Deglaze the pan with the vinegar, scraping up and mixing in any browned bits stuck to the bottom. Bring to a simmer, still over medium-high heat, and cook until the liquid has thickened and reduced by about two-thirds.

3. Transfer to the slow cooker and add the stock and rosemary sprigs. Cover and cook on high for 4 hours or on low for 8 hours, until the meat is fall-off-the-bone tender.

4. Transfer the ribs to a serving platter and cover to keep warm. Remove the rosemary sprigs from the cooker and discard. Transfer the liquid to a medium saucepan and bring to a simmer over high heat. In a glass, whisk together the cornstarch and cold water to create a slurry. Stir the slurry into the saucepan and simmer, whisking constantly until the sauce has thickened, 2 to 3 minutes. Taste and add more salt, if desired. Pour the shallot gravy over the short ribs, garnish with parsley, and serve.

TIPS & NOTES

- *Serve over a bed of Garlic-Herb Mashed Potatoes (page 189), creamy polenta, or rice to soak up the rich, flavorful gravy.*

- *In place of balsamic vinegar, you can swap in a dry red wine or a combination of red wine and apple cider vinegar for a deeper, more complex flavor.*

- *To make it a full meal, add carrots, parsnips, or potatoes to the slow cooker during the last 2 hours of cooking.*

MISSISSIPPI POT ROAST

SERVES: **6**

PREP TIME: **10 MINUTES**

COOK TIME: **6 TO 8 HOURS**

1 (3- to 4-pound) chuck roast

1 (1-ounce) packet ranch seasoning mix

1 (1-ounce) packet brown gravy mix

6 tablespoons salted butter

6 pepperoncini, thinly sliced, plus ¼ cup brine from the pepperoncini jar

6 large cloves garlic

2 tablespoons dried minced onion

1. Preheat the slow cooker on the low setting.

2. Trim the excess fat from the chuck roast. Place the roast in the slow cooker and sprinkle the ranch seasoning and gravy mix over it. Top with the butter, pepperoncini peppers and juice, garlic, and dried onion. Cover and cook on low for 6 to 8 hours, until the roast is tender and easily shreds with a fork. Use two forks to shred the meat right in the juices.

TIPS & NOTES

- *For deeper flavor, brown the chuck roast in olive oil in a skillet over medium-high heat to form a nice crust on all sides before adding to the slow cooker.*

- *While chuck roast is ideal for this recipe due to its marbling, you can also use brisket, shoulder roast, or round roast.*

- *Trim the excess fat from the roast before cooking to prevent the meat from being too greasy. Some marbling is good, but too much fat can make the finished dish oily and flavorless.*

- *Make it a complete meal by adding large chunks of carrots, potatoes, and onions to the slow cooker about 2 hours before the roast is finished.*

- *This is also delicious served on top of Garlic-Herb Mashed Potatoes (page 189).*

SWEDISH MEATBALLS

SERVES: **4**

PREP TIME: **20 MINUTES**

COOK TIME: **4 TO 6 HOURS**

FOR THE MEATBALLS

1 pound ground beef

1 pound ground pork

½ cup panko breadcrumbs

2 tablespoons chopped fresh flat-leaf parsley, plus extra for garnish

2 teaspoons sea salt

½ teaspoon black pepper

1 teaspoon onion powder

1 teaspoon garlic powder

½ teaspoon allspice

½ teaspoon ground nutmeg

2 large eggs

2 tablespoons olive oil

FOR THE SAUCE

2 cups beef stock

⅔ cup heavy cream

2 tablespoons Worcestershire sauce

1 tablespoon Dijon mustard

3 tablespoons cornstarch

3 tablespoons cold water

½ cup sour cream

1. Put the ground beef, ground pork, panko, parsley, salt, pepper, onion powder, garlic powder, allspice, nutmeg, and eggs in a large mixing bowl and mix with your hands until the ingredients are well combined. Form the mixture into 35 to 40 meatballs about 1½ inches in diameter.

2. Heat the olive oil in a large skillet over medium-high heat. Working in batches, add the meatballs and brown them on all sides, 5 to 7 minutes per batch. You're looking for a nice crust on the outside without cooking them all the way through. Transfer the browned meatballs to the slow cooker.

3. Make the sauce: In a medium bowl, whisk together the stock, cream, Worcestershire sauce, and mustard. Pour the sauce over the meatballs in the slow cooker.

4. Cover and cook on low for 4 to 5 hours or on high 2 to 3 hours.

5. In a small bowl, whisk together the cornstarch and cold water to create a slurry. Stir the slurry into the sauce in the slow cooker. Cover and cook for 30 minutes to 1 hour longer, until the sauce has thickened. Stir in the sour cream until well incorporated. Taste and add more salt and pepper, if desired. Garnish with parsley and serve.

TIPS & NOTES

- *I like to serve these meatballs with Garlic-Herb Mashed Potatoes (page 189), peas, and a little bit of lingonberry jam. They are also delicious over wide egg noodles.*

- *To adapt this recipe for the stovetop, brown the meatballs in a large skillet as directed. Remove and set aside. In the same pan, whisk together the stock, cream, Worcestershire sauce, and mustard. Bring to a simmer over medium heat. Return the meatballs to the skillet, cover, and cook, stirring occasionally, for 20 to 25 minutes. Add the cornstarch slurry, cook for another 5 minutes, until thickened, and finish with the sour cream before serving.*

KICKIN' CHILI

2½ pounds ground beef

1 medium red onion, chopped

5 cloves garlic, minced

3 large ribs celery, diced

¼ cup pickled jalapeño slices, chopped

1 (14.5-ounce) can tomatoes and green chilies, with juices

1 (14.5-ounce) can stewed tomatoes, with juices

1 (6-ounce) can tomato paste

2 tablespoons Worcestershire sauce

¼ cup chili powder

3 tablespoons unsweetened cocoa powder

2 heaping tablespoons ground cumin

2 teaspoons sea salt

1 teaspoon black pepper

1 teaspoon garlic powder

1 teaspoon onion powder

1 teaspoon dried oregano

½ teaspoon cayenne pepper

1 bay leaf

FOR SERVING

Shredded cheddar cheese

Sour cream

Tortilla chips

Sliced green onions

1. Preheat the slow cooker on the low setting.

2. In a large skillet over medium-high heat, combine the ground beef, onion, and garlic and cook until the beef is browned, 8 to 10 minutes. Drain the excess grease.

3. Transfer the ground beef mixture to the slow cooker. Add the celery, jalapeños, tomatoes and chilies (with liquid), stewed tomatoes (with liquid), tomato paste, Worcestershire sauce, chili powder, cocoa powder, cumin, salt, black pepper, garlic powder, onion powder, oregano, cayenne, and bay leaf. Stir until the ingredients are well combined. Cover and cook on low for 6 to 8 hours.

4. Serve with cheddar cheese, sour cream, tortilla chips, and sliced green onions.

> **TIPS & NOTES**
>
> - *If you enjoy beans in your chili, stir in a can or two of drained kidney beans, black beans, or pinto beans during the last hour of cooking.*
>
> - *This chili is excellent for meal prep as it freezes well. Let cool completely, portion into freezer-safe bags or containers, and freeze for up to 3 months. Thaw in the fridge overnight and reheat on the stovetop.*
>
> - *To adapt this recipe for the stovetop, brown the ground beef, onion, and garlic in a large pot over medium-high heat, then drain the excess grease. Add the celery, jalapeños, tomatoes and chilies, stewed tomatoes, tomato paste, Worcestershire sauce, and all of the spices and stir well. Bring to a boil, then reduce the heat to low, cover, and simmer for 1½ to 2 hours, stirring occasionally.*

PULLED PORK

4½ pounds boneless pork shoulder or pork butt

1 tablespoon plus 1 teaspoon smoked paprika

1 tablespoon sea salt

2 teaspoons ground cumin

1½ teaspoons dried oregano

1 teaspoon dry mustard

1 teaspoon chili powder

1 teaspoon dried thyme

1 teaspoon black pepper

1 medium yellow onion, diced

6 cloves garlic, chopped

Juice of 1 large orange

1. Preheat the slow cooker on the low setting.

2. Trim the excess fat from the pork and pat the pork dry. In a small mixing bowl, combine the paprika, salt, cumin, oregano, dry mustard, chili powder, thyme, and pepper. Rub the seasoning mixture over the entire pork shoulder.

3. Put the seasoned pork in the slow cooker and top with the onion, garlic, and orange juice. Cover and cook on low for 8 hours, until the meat is fall-apart tender. Use two forks to shred the meat directly in the slow cooker.

4. Use a slotted spoon to transfer the pulled pork to a serving dish. Spoon some of the juice from the slow cooker over the meat before serving.

TIPS & NOTES

- *Orange juice adds a nice zesty touch to balance the richness of the pork. For a different twist, you could use pineapple juice, apple cider vinegar, or even lime juice for a tangier flavor.*

- *If you find the pulled pork too dry after shredding, add a bit of the leftover juice from the slow cooker or a splash of chicken broth to moisten it.*

- *Add a touch of brown sugar or maple syrup to the seasoning mixture for a hint of sweetness that balances the spice.*

PORK CHOPS with CARROTS and MUSHROOMS

SERVES: **4**

PREP TIME: **20 MINUTES**

COOK TIME: **6 HOURS**

1½ cups chicken stock

2 teaspoons sherry vinegar

3 tablespoons all-purpose flour

4 medium carrots (about 12 ounces), peeled and cut into 2-inch pieces

10 ounces shiitake mushrooms, stems removed and caps halved

1 small yellow onion, sliced

3 cloves garlic, minced

4 fresh thyme sprigs

2 fresh oregano sprigs

4 (10-ounce) thick-cut, bone-in pork chops

1 teaspoon sea salt

¾ teaspoon black pepper

2 tablespoons olive oil

⅓ cup dry white wine

3 tablespoons heavy cream

6 ounces wide egg noodles, cooked according to package directions

2 teaspoons fresh thyme leaves, for garnish

1. Preheat the slow cooker on the low setting.

2. Put the stock, vinegar, and flour in the slow cooker and whisk to combine. Stir in the carrots, mushrooms, onion, garlic, thyme, and oregano. Cover.

3. Season the pork chops on both sides with the salt and pepper. Heat the olive oil in a large skillet over medium-high heat. Sear the chops until they are nicely caramelized on both sides, 2 to 3 minutes per side. Transfer the pork chops to the slow cooker.

4. Deglaze the pan with the wine, scraping up and mixing in any browned bits stuck to the bottom. Pour the wine mixture over the pork chops and vegetables. Cover and cook on low for 5 to 6 hours or on high for 3 to 4 hours. Remove the chops from the slow cooker and keep warm. Discard the herb sprigs.

5. Mix the cream and cooked egg noodles into the sauce in the slow cooker and toss to combine. Taste and add more salt and pepper, if desired.

6. Plate the pork chops and vegetables over the noodles, drizzle with the remaining sauce from the slow cooker, and garnish with the thyme leaves.

TIPS & NOTES

- *Searing Matters: Don't skip the searing! That golden crust adds a deep, savory layer to the final dish that slow cooking alone can't achieve. Get the pan nice and hot before you start.*

- *Deglazing = Flavor Boost: When you pour in the wine to deglaze, really scrape up all those little browned bits stuck to the skillet. They're flavor gold.*

- *Herb Swap: No fresh herbs? Use ½ teaspoon dried thyme and ½ teaspoon dried oregano instead. Add them along with the vegetables in Step 2.*

TERIYAKI CHICKEN

2 pounds boneless, skinless chicken thighs, trimmed

5 cloves garlic, minced

1 tablespoon plus 1 teaspoon freshly grated ginger

¾ cup soy sauce

⅓ cup honey

¼ cup packed brown sugar

3 tablespoons unseasoned rice vinegar

1 tablespoon toasted sesame oil

¼ cup cold water

2 tablespoons cornstarch

2 green onions, sliced on a bias, for garnish

1 tablespoon toasted sesame seeds, for garnish

1. Place the chicken thighs in the slow cooker.

2. In a small bowl, whisk together the garlic, ginger, soy sauce, honey, brown sugar, rice vinegar, and sesame oil. Pour the mixture over the chicken in the slow cooker. Cover and cook on high for 3 to 4 hours or on low for 6 to 7 hours, until the chicken is cooked all the way through and nearly fall-apart tender.

3. Transfer the chicken to a cutting board and cut into bite-size pieces.

4. Strain the juices from the slow cooker into a large skillet. Bring to a boil over medium-high heat, then reduce to a simmer. In a small bowl, whisk together the water and cornstarch to create a slurry. Stir the slurry into the skillet and simmer for 2 minutes, or until the sauce has just started to thicken. Add the chicken and toss until it is evenly coated in the sauce. Serve garnished with the green onions and sesame seeds.

TIPS & NOTES

- *For a complete meal, toss in some broccoli florets, bell peppers, and snap peas during the last 30 minutes of cooking.*

- *You can also serve the chicken with sautéed bok choy, broccoli, or green beans on the side.*

- *For a spicy kick, add sriracha, red pepper flakes, or crispy garlic chili oil to the sauce.*

- *For a sweet and tangy take, add fresh or canned pineapple chunks during the last 20 minutes of cooking.*

LENTIL and ITALIAN SAUSAGE SOUP

SERVES: **6 TO 8**

PREP TIME: **25 MINUTES**

COOK TIME: **6 TO 8 HOURS**

1½ cups green lentils, thoroughly rinsed

5 cups chicken stock

1½ pounds ground Italian sausage

2 tablespoons salted butter

2 tablespoons olive oil

1 cup baby spinach leaves, packed

¾ cup diced carrots

¾ cup diced onion

4 cloves garlic, minced

1 small leek, cleaned, trimmed, and diced

2 ribs celery, diced

Sea salt and black pepper

1½ cups heavy cream

¾ cup finely grated Parmesan cheese

2 tablespoons Dijon mustard

2 tablespoons red wine vinegar

1. Preheat the slow cooker on the low setting. Put the lentils and stock in the slow cooker.

2. In a large skillet over medium-high heat, cook the sausage in the butter and olive oil until browned, about 8 minutes. Using a slotted spoon, transfer the sausage to the slow cooker, reserving the drippings in the skillet.

3. Add the spinach, carrots, onion, garlic, leek, celery, and a little salt and pepper to the skillet and sauté over medium heat until the vegetables are tender, about 10 minutes.

4. Using a slotted spoon, transfer the sautéed vegetables to the slow cooker and mix into the sausage. Stir in the cream, Parmesan cheese, mustard, and vinegar. Cover and cook on low for 6 to 8 hours, until the lentils are tender and the soup is thick.

TIPS & NOTES

- *Leeks can trap dirt between their layers, so it's important to clean them thoroughly. Start by cutting off the dark green tops (you can save them for making stock) and trimming the root end. Slice the leek lengthwise, then fan the layers open under running water to rinse out any dirt or grit. You can also slice the leek into half-moons and soak the pieces in a bowl of water, gently agitating them to loosen the dirt before draining.*

- *To make this soup on the stovetop, brown the sausage in a large stockpot or Dutch oven, then sauté all of the vegetables except the spinach in the sausage drippings until tender. Drain the excess grease. Add the stock and rinsed lentils, bring to a boil, and simmer for 25 to 30 minutes, until the lentils are tender. Stir in the spinach, cream, Parmesan, mustard, and vinegar and cook for another 10 to 15 minutes, until the flavors have come together and the soup has thickened.*

GARLIC-HERB MASHED POTATOES

SERVES: **8**

PREP TIME: **20 MINUTES**

COOK TIME: **3 TO 7 HOURS**

1½ pounds red potatoes, scrubbed, cut into small cubes

1½ pounds Yukon Gold potatoes, peeled and cut into small cubes

1 cup chicken stock or vegetable stock

6 tablespoons salted butter, cut into cubes, or more to taste

4 cloves garlic, minced

½ cup heavy cream, warmed, or more to taste

½ cup sour cream

2 tablespoons chopped fresh chives, plus extra for garnish

1 tablespoon chopped fresh flat-leaf parsley, plus extra for garnish

1 teaspoon chopped fresh dill, plus extra for garnish

1 teaspoon sea salt

½ teaspoon black pepper

Pinch of red pepper flakes

1. Put the potatoes, stock, butter, and garlic in the slow cooker. Cover and cook on high for 3 to 4 hours or on low for 6 to 7 hours, until the potatoes are soft.

2. Using a potato masher or an electric mixer, mash the potatoes. Add the heavy cream, sour cream, chives, parsley, dill, salt, pepper, and red pepper flakes. Mash again until the potatoes have reached your desired consistency. Taste and add more salt and pepper, if desired. If the potatoes are not creamy enough, add more cream and butter until they have reached the desired level of creaminess.

3. Garnish with additional herbs and serve.

TIPS & NOTES

- *To make on the stovetop, place the cubed potatoes in a large pot, cover with cold water, and add 1 teaspoon of salt. Bring to a boil, reduce the heat, and simmer until the potatoes are tender, 15 to 20 minutes. Drain well. Add the butter, garlic, and cream directly to the hot potatoes and mash with the other ingredients as directed.*

- FLAVOR VARIATIONS

  - **Cheesy Mashed Potatoes:** *Fold in 1 cup shredded cheddar or Parmesan cheese.*

  - **Loaded Mashed Potatoes***: Top with crispy bacon, shredded cheddar cheese, and a dollop of sour cream. Garnish with chives.*

  - **Roasted Garlic Mashed Potatoes:** *Replace the minced garlic with 1 head of Whole Roasted Garlic (page 311), squeezing out the cloves and mashing them into the potatoes with the cream and seasonings.*

  - **Truffle Mashed Potatoes:** *Add 1 teaspoon truffle oil and top with freshly grated Parmesan.*

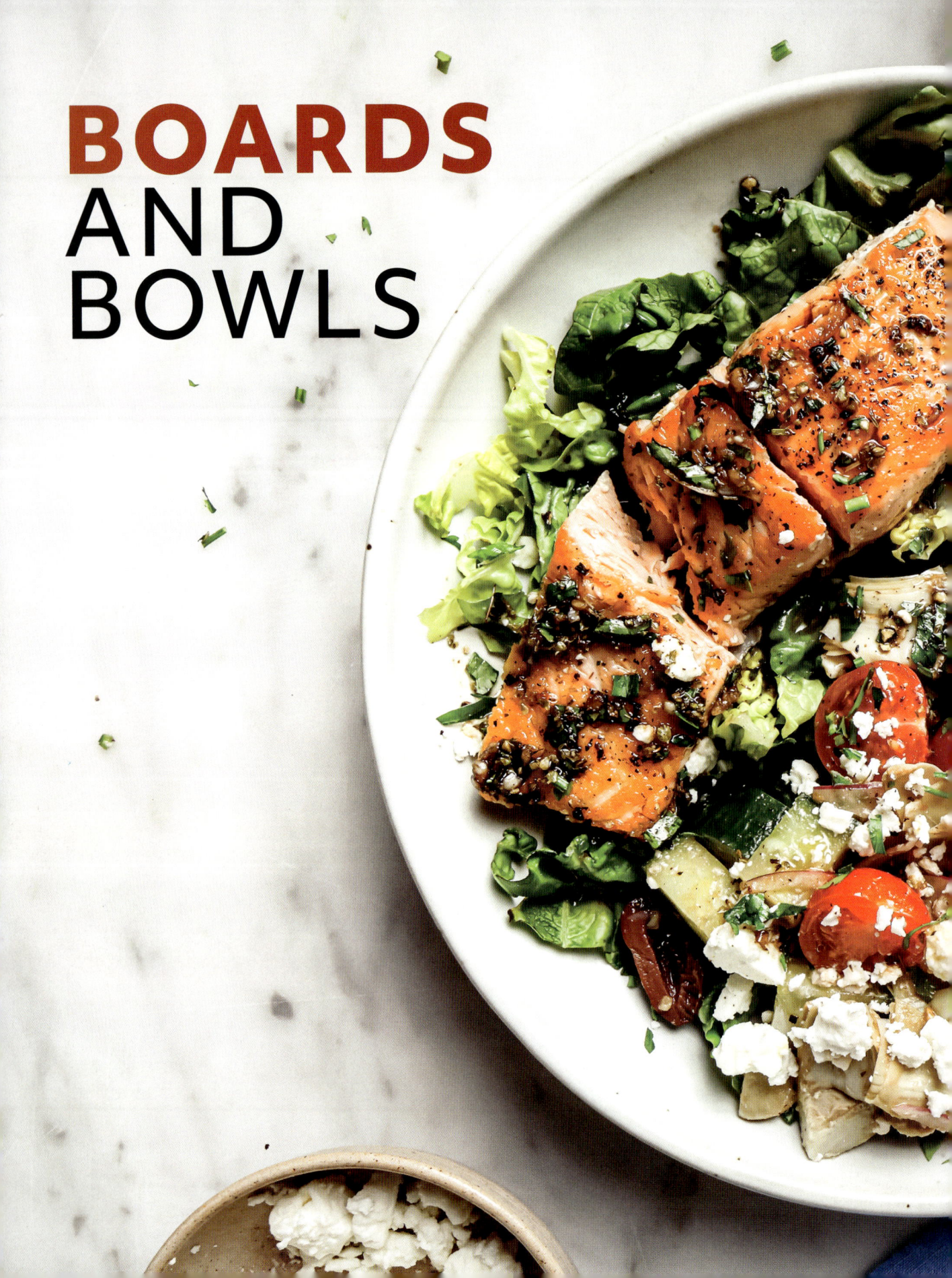

BOARDS
AND
BOWLS

Both bowls and boards have a unique way of blending flavors, textures, and vibrant colors to make a truly show-stopping presentation. Which is perfect because, after all, you eat with your eyes first.

Bowls are the perfect vessel for creating vibrant, fresh salads or hearty protein combos, with ingredients coming together to form a balanced, satisfying meal. Boards, on the other hand, allow for an interactive dining experience, where guests can explore an assortment of thoughtfully curated ingredients while essentially still choosing their own meal.

Whether you're tossing together a hearty salad, layering a protein bowl, or crafting a visually stunning grazing spread, bowls and boards offer endless opportunities for variety and creativity.

BOWLS: a SYMPHONY of DIVERSE INGREDIENTS

A salad can easily morph from a light, refreshing side to a hearty main event with the addition of the right combination of ingredients.

A protein bowl is a meal in itself, loaded with a variety of colors, textures, and flavors, each element working with the next to create the perfect bite. There's an art to layering a bowl, using a combination of grains, leafy greens, roasted vegetables, and/or a protein, then drizzling with a sauce or dressing to bring it all together. Understanding how to build your bowl is all about choosing the right base and building layers of texture and flavor.

Base: Every great bowl starts with a foundation. When selecting a base, think about the desired texture and heaviness of the meal. Lighter options like leafy greens (romaine, arugula, kale, spinach) make for refreshing, crisp bowls, while whole grains (quinoa, farro, brown rice), beans, and/or roasted vegetables add substance and heartiness, making them perfect for heavier meals.

Protein: This is where you can really get creative. Roasted chicken, grilled steak, seared salmon, grilled shrimp, and plant-based proteins like chickpeas or tofu are all great options. Add depth of flavor by roasting, grilling, or pan-searing the protein (or vegetables) and make sure to season well, or consider marinating them ahead of time to allow the flavors to penetrate. Try to match the flavor profile of the protein with the rest of your ingredients. This could be a smoky, spiced chicken paired with fresh greens and avocado, or a simple grilled salmon over a bed of rice with roasted vegetables.

Texture: Here's where bowls really come to life. Don't be afraid to play with contrasts: think a hearty grain, tender roasted vegetables, fresh raw greens, soft crumbled cheese, and roasted meat, finished with a creamy sauce drizzled over the top. Toasted nuts and seeds or other toppings like Crispy Garlic Chickpeas (page 84) or croutons can provide a satisfying crunch to complement softer elements.

Sauce or dressing: The finishing touch to any great bowl is the sauce or dressing. This is where you tie the dish together. From bold sauces and dressings to lighter vinaigrettes, a perfectly paired sauce is like the icing on the cake. A simple drizzle of oil and vinegar, or a spoonful of hummus can work wonders too.

BOARDS: ELEVATING the SHARED MEAL

Boards bring together an array of ingredients that are meant to be shared but also personalized. Whether you're putting together a burger bar, a salad spread, or a breakfast board, the key is balancing sweet and savory, crunchy and creamy, warm and cold. The beauty of a well curated spread is that it's a feast for both the eyes and the taste buds, and it can showcase a variety of textures, colors, and flavors that ensures no two bites are the same.

Creative combinations: Start with a base: Depending on the category, it could be a selection of crackers or bread, sliced vegetables, hearty lettuce. Then think about adding a mix of proteins, spreads and cheeses, and fruit. For example, on a pancake board, fluffy pancakes sit alongside bacon and sausage, along with syrups, whipped cream, and a variety of toppings like nuts, granola, berries, and chocolate chips. On a bagel board, you can offer an assortment of bagels with smoked salmon and hard-boiled eggs, along with different spreads like flavored cream cheeses and toppings like capers, pickled onion, microgreens, and tomatoes, creating a customizable experience for all your guests.

Assembly and presentation: Group similar items but leave space to let each element shine. Arrange flavorful and textured elements in such a way that they complement each other, like soft cheeses near crispy crackers, or sweet fruits alongside salty meats. Use small bowls to house dips, spreads, nuts, and olives to create focal points. If you're incorporating meats and cheeses, think about creating variety across the board, so the flavors feel balanced as guests move from one section to the next.

Warm versus cold: Many items on your board will naturally be served cold, like sliced meats, cheeses, and fresh fruit. However, you can also incorporate warm elements for contrast. Consider adding a warm bread, roasted vegetables, or grilled meats for a contrast in temperatures. And keep in mind that if your board features a hot component, like the Chili Charcuterie board (page 202), plan ahead for heating and storage so that the warm items can be held at the right temperature throughout the meal.

Substitutions: One of the greatest benefits of boards is their flexibility. Feel free to experiment and swap out ingredients based on dietary restrictions, seasonal availability, or whatever you have on hand.

TIPS and TRICKS

Batch cooking: For bowls, batch-cook grains, proteins, and vegetables in advance. Store each ingredient in its own storage container and then build different bowls throughout the week based on what sounds good.

Pre-assembled options: For boards, consider buying presliced meats, cheeses, and fresh produce to cut down on prep time. Many grocery stores offer trays of cut vegetables, fruits, and ready-to-eat deli meats, which can speed up the process significantly.

Create a flavor profile: Whether for a bowl or a board, focus on creating the flavor profile and vibe you want. For example, the Burger Board (page 204) is basically a DIY burger bar, but all of the components make sense together and complement each other. The same is true of the other spreads throughout the chapter—something to entice all palates, with a mix of cohesive ingredients. Understanding how flavors play off each other makes assembling both bowls and boards a seamless and enjoyable experience.

Make it user-friendly: For boards, provide tools like tongs, spoons, and mini spatulas for guests to serve themselves. This encourages sharing and interaction and can make the meal feel more festive and communal. It's also nice to not have everyone grabbing the food with their possibly germy hands.

Bowls and boards are more than just meals; they're an invitation to get creative in the kitchen. Whether you're assembling a hearty protein bowl or designing a burger board that has a little something for everyone, these dishes are fully customizable, offering endless opportunities to experiment.

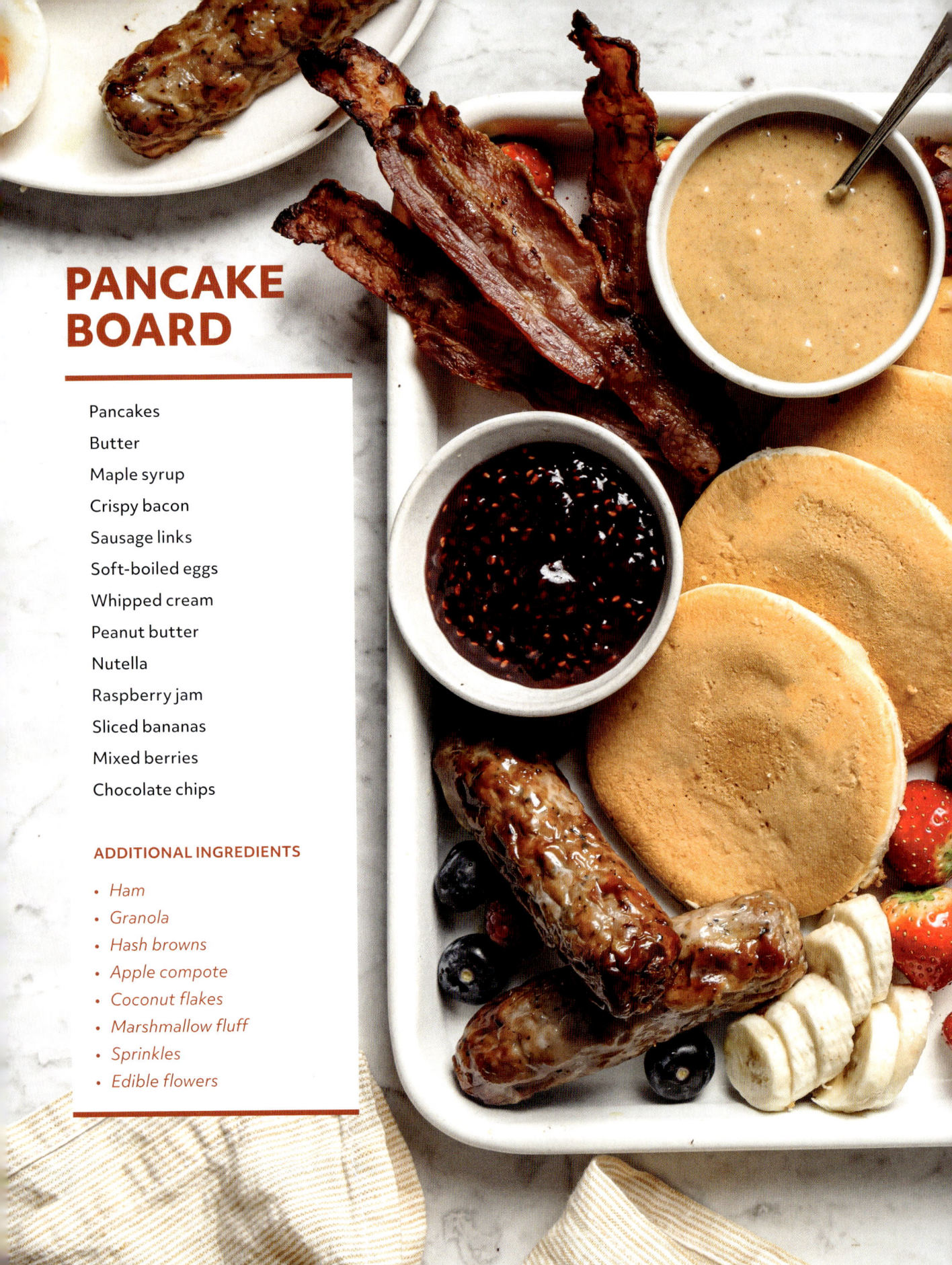

PANCAKE BOARD

Pancakes

Butter

Maple syrup

Crispy bacon

Sausage links

Soft-boiled eggs

Whipped cream

Peanut butter

Nutella

Raspberry jam

Sliced bananas

Mixed berries

Chocolate chips

ADDITIONAL INGREDIENTS

- *Ham*
- *Granola*
- *Hash browns*
- *Apple compote*
- *Coconut flakes*
- *Marshmallow fluff*
- *Sprinkles*
- *Edible flowers*

BAGEL BOARD

Everything bagels (or a variety of bagels)

Whipped cream cheese

Lox

Pesto

Jammy soft-boiled eggs

Sliced prosciutto

Sliced fresh mozzarella cheese

Sliced avocado

Mixed olives

Capers

Sliced watermelon radishes

Sliced English cucumber

Sliced heirloom tomatoes

Arugula

Microgreens

Pickled red onions

Chopped fresh chives

Fresh dill

Small fresh basil leaves

Lemon slices

ADDITIONAL INGREDIENTS

- *Burrata*
- *Brie*
- *Smoked trout*
- *Olive Salad (page 308)*
- *Sliced pear*
- *Figs*
- *Hummus*
- *Sun-dried tomatoes*
- *Sliced beets*

WEDGE SPREAD

Iceberg lettuce wedges

Ranch dressing

Blue cheese crumbles

Crispy bacon bits

Cubed avocado

Candied walnuts

Roma tomatoes

Sliced red onion

Chopped fresh chives

Cracked black pepper

ADDITIONAL INGREDIENTS

- *Roasted Blackened Chicken and Vegetables (page 66)*
- *Garlic Butter Steak Bites (page 95)*
- *Grilled shrimp*
- *Hard-boiled eggs*
- *Onion straws*
- *Cucumber*
- *Croutons*

CHILI CHARCUTERIE

Kickin' Chili (page 178)

Grilled hot dogs and buns

Shredded Mexican blend cheese

Crackers

Tortilla chips

Fritos

Sour cream

Cubed avocado

Crispy bacon bits

Sliced black olives

Diced tomatoes

Sweet corn

Finely chopped red onion

Sliced green onions

Sliced jalapeños

Chopped fresh cilantro

ADDITIONAL INGREDIENTS

- *Cornbread*
- *Baked potatoes*
- *Tortillas*
- *French fries*
- *Fried onion rings*
- *Sautéed bell peppers*
- *Pico de gallo*
- *Pickled red onions*
- *Cilantro*

BURGER BOARD

Grilled cheeseburger patties

Brioche burger buns

Crispy bacon

Fried eggs

Sliced avocado

Caramelized onions

Sautéed mushrooms

Butter lettuce

Sliced beefsteak tomatoes

Pickles

Sliced jalapeños

Sliced red onion

Burger Sauce (page 305)

Ketchup

Mustard

Mayonnaise

ADDITIONAL INGREDIENTS

- *Veggie burgers*
- *Chicken burgers*
- *Onion rings*
- *French fries*
- *Blue cheese crumbles*
- *Pineapple slices*
- *Coleslaw*
- *Barbecue sauce*

KALE, SPINACH, and ROMAINE CAESAR

2½ ounces baby kale

2½ ounces baby spinach

5 ounces romaine lettuce, chopped

1 cup shaved Parmesan cheese, divided

Caesar Dressing (page 305)

1 cup Crispy Garlic Chickpeas (page 84)

Cracked black pepper (optional)

Lemon wedges, for serving

1. In a large mixing bowl, toss the kale, spinach, romaine, and half of the Parmesan. Add the desired amount of dressing and toss again until all of the greens are evenly coated.

2. Top with the remaining Parmesan and the crispy chickpeas. Garnish with cracked black pepper, if desired, and serve with lemon wedges.

> **TIPS & NOTES**
>
> - *Add a protein like crab, grilled shrimp, blackened salmon, or roasted chicken.*
>
> - *Some of my favorite add-ins for this salad include avocado, roasted vegetables, pepitas, pomegranate seeds, chopped apples or pears, and blue cheese crumbles—and of course we can't forget bacon.*

CHIMICHURRI CHICKEN SALAD BOWLS

¼ cup chimichurri

2 tablespoons balsamic vinegar

2 heads baby gem or butter lettuce, roughly chopped (6 to 8 cups)

10 ounces cooked chicken, cubed or shredded

1 large avocado, peeled, pitted, and thinly sliced

½ cup quartered grape tomatoes

½ cup canned chickpeas, drained and rinsed

½ cup quartered marinated artichoke hearts

⅓ cup crumbled goat cheese

¼ cup sliced pepperoncini

¼ cup thinly sliced pickled red onion

2 tablespoons sunflower seeds

1. Make the dressing: In a small bowl, whisk together the chimichurri and balsamic.

2. Divide the lettuce evenly between two bowls. Divide the remaining ingredients evenly between the bowls. Drizzle the desired amount of dressing over each salad, or serve the dressing on the side.

TIPS & NOTES

- *This recipe is an excellent way to use up leftover Lemon-Herb Roasted Chicken (page 145) or Herbed Butter Spatchcocked Chicken (page 64).*

- *For some added crunch, replace the canned chickpeas with Crispy Garlic Chickpeas (page 84).*

- *This is one of my favorite recipes to meal prep, storing all of the prepped ingredients separately to create my own personal salad bar.*

CALIFORNIA ROLL in a BOWL

SERVES: **2**

PREP TIME: **20 MINUTES**

COOK TIME: **15 MINUTES**

2 tablespoons unseasoned rice vinegar

2 teaspoons sugar

¼ teaspoon sea salt

2 cups cooked sushi rice

8 ounces imitation crab meat (surimi), cut into bite-size pieces

1 medium avocado, peeled, pitted, and cubed

4 dried seaweed snack sheets, crumbled, or 1 nori sheet, sliced

½ cup chopped English or Persian cucumber

½ cup shredded carrots

FOR SERVING

Yum Yum Sauce (page 306)

1 tablespoon toasted black and white sesame seeds

Soy sauce

Pickled ginger

Wasabi paste

1. Whisk together the rice vinegar, sugar, and salt in a mixing bowl. Add the cooked rice and toss to combine.

2. Divide the rice between two serving bowls. Arrange half of the crab meat, avocado, seaweed, cucumber, and carrots in each bowl.

3. Drizzle some yum yum sauce over the tops, then sprinkle on the sesame seeds. Serve with soy sauce, pickled ginger, and wasabi on the side.

TIPS & NOTES

- *For a different protein option, this dish is also delicious with real crab, cooked shrimp, flaked salmon, or even tofu.*

- *Homemade sauces are always better, but if you're pressed for time, you can buy premade yum yum sauce.*

- *Add edamame, sliced radishes, or thinly sliced bell peppers for an extra serving of vegetables.*

- *Top the bowls with crispy tempura crumbs, toasted panko, or crushed rice crackers for added crunch.*

GREEK SALMON BOWLS

FOR THE DRESSING

¼ cup plus 2 tablespoons olive oil

3 tablespoons balsamic vinegar

4 cloves garlic, minced

2 tablespoons chopped fresh flat-leaf parsley

2 teaspoons dried oregano

FOR THE SALMON

4 (6-ounce) skinless salmon fillets

Sea salt and black pepper

2 tablespoons olive oil

FOR THE SALAD

6 cups chopped romaine lettuce

1 cucumber, diced

1 cup halved cherry tomatoes

½ small red onion, thinly sliced

⅓ cup halved pitted Kalamata olives

1 cup quartered marinated artichoke hearts

1 large avocado, peeled, pitted, and sliced

⅔ cup crumbled feta cheese

Lemon wedges, for serving

1. Make the dressing: Put all of the ingredients in a small bowl and whisk until well combined.

2. Cook the salmon: Season the salmon fillets generously with salt and pepper. Heat the olive oil in a large nonstick skillet over medium heat. Place the fillets in the pan and cook for about 4 minutes per side, until the salmon is golden brown and cooked through, or to the desired level of doneness.

3. Toss the salad: Combine the lettuce, cucumber, tomatoes, red onion, olives, and artichoke hearts in a large bowl. Toss with half of the dressing until the ingredients are evenly coated.

4. Divide the salad evenly among four bowls. Top each with a piece of salmon, avocado slices, and crumbled feta. Drizzle over some of the remaining dressing and serve with lemon wedges.

TIPS & NOTES

- *For more crunch, top with toasted pine nuts, pumpkin seeds, or crushed pita chips.*

- *Not a fan of salmon? This bowl is also excellent with grilled chicken, octopus, or shrimp.*

- *Add some Cucumber Sauce (page 307) or hummus for an extra Mediterranean twist.*

UMAMI BEEF BOWLS

SERVES: **2**

PREP TIME: **15 MINUTES, PLUS TIME TO MARINATE**

COOK TIME: **15 MINUTES**

1½ pounds New York strip steak

½ cup coconut aminos

4 cloves garlic, minced

2 tablespoons dried minced onion

1½ teaspoons sea salt

1 teaspoon black pepper

2 tablespoons olive oil

2 cups cooked rice, for serving

1 tablespoon toasted sesame seeds, for garnish

1. Place the steak in a glass food storage container with a lid. Pour the coconut aminos over the top and add the dried onion, garlic, salt, and pepper. Put the lid on and shake well to mix. Place in the fridge and marinate for 24 to 48 hours, shaking a couple of times a day to mix the marinade and make sure the meat is evenly coated.

2. Remove the steak from the marinade, retaining the marinade. Slice the steak against the grain into ¼-inch-thick slices. Return the steak strips to the marinade and toss.

3. Heat the olive oil in a large skillet over medium-high heat. Working in two batches if necessary (to get a nice sear on the meat, avoid overcrowding the pan), sear the meat for 1 to 2 minutes on each side.

4. Serve with the rice and your favorite green vegetable. Garnish with the sesame seeds.

TIPS & NOTES

- *For a little kick, add some red pepper flakes or sriracha to the marinade. Even better, top the finished dish with crispy garlic chili oil.*

- *For a bright, herbaceous finish, top with loads of fresh herbs like cilantro or chives, or sliced green onions.*

- *My favorite way to cook broccoli for a dish like this is in the air fryer. I cook it exactly like I cook the Umami Brussels Sprouts (page 259), which are also excellent with this beef.*

HOISIN BEEF BOWLS

SERVES: **4**

PREP TIME: **15 MINUTES**

COOK TIME: **20 MINUTES**

1 tablespoon toasted sesame oil

2 pounds ground beef

4 green onions, sliced on a bias, green and white parts separated

4 cloves garlic, chopped

1 tablespoon freshly grated ginger

¼ cup plus 2 tablespoons hoisin sauce

3 tablespoons soy sauce

2 tablespoons tomato paste

1 tablespoon packed brown sugar

2 teaspoons sriracha or chili paste

4 cups cooked rice, for serving

1 red bell pepper, seeded and julienned

1 small carrot, julienned

½ small head purple cabbage, thinly shredded

⅓ cup chopped cashews, for garnish

2 tablespoons toasted sesame seeds, for garnish

1. Heat the sesame oil in a large skillet over medium-high heat. Add the ground beef and cook, using a wooden spoon to break it up as it cooks. Add the white parts of the green onions, the garlic, and ginger and continue cooking until the meat is fully browned, about 10 minutes total. Drain the excess grease.

2. In a small bowl, whisk together the hoisin sauce, soy sauce, tomato paste, brown sugar, and sriracha until the ingredients are well incorporated. Add the sauce to the meat, mix, and cook until warmed through.

3. Divide the rice among four bowls. Arrange the beef on top of the rice, then the bell pepper, carrots, and cabbage alongside the beef. Garnish with the green parts of the onion, the cashews, and sesame seeds and serve.

TIPS & NOTES

- *Ground beef is traditional in this recipe, but you can use ground turkey, chicken, or pork for a lighter version.*

- *The vegetables in this dish add great texture and crunch. Feel free to swap the bell pepper, carrots, or cabbage with other veggies like cucumber, snap peas, or shredded zucchini if desired.*

- *This recipe is great for meal prep! You can cook the beef mixture ahead of time, store it separately from the rice and veggies, and assemble the bowls when ready to serve.*

- *For a noodle-based version, serve the hoisin beef over rice noodles or soba noodles instead of rice.*

TOASTS

Toast has long been the humble hero of breakfast, late-night snacking, and everything in between. I have been known on multiple occasions to make a meal out of toasted croissant bread with salted butter. It's time to transform toast from a simple breakfast side to a full meal deal.

Making a gourmet, bougie toast isn't just about the bread; it's about layering flavor and texture with each topping to create something as unique as it is delicious. Whether you're hosting a brunch with friends, looking to level up your own breakfast game, or simply want a delicious meal any time of day, the toast recipes in this chapter are sure to become part of your permanent rotation.

BUILDING the PERFECT TOAST

 STEP 1 ## CHOOSE YOUR BREAD

The bread is your foundation. Think about the flavor, texture, and overall taste you are going for. Do you want something hearty and rustic or soft and buttery?

- **Sourdough:** Tangy and chewy
- **Croissant loaf:** Flaky, crispy, and chewy
- **Brioche or challah:** Soft, rich, and slightly sweet
- **Whole-grain/seeded bread:** Nutty, earthy, and sturdy
- **Ciabatta or rustic country loaf:** Airy but crusty

Pro Tip: Slice the bread about ¾ inch thick to balance crispiness and chew. Too thin can result in soggy toast under the weight of the toppings, and too thick can lead to a dry, underwhelming bite.

 STEP 2 ## TOAST TO PERFECTION

How you toast your bread matters. The goal is golden edges, a crisp exterior, and a warm, slightly chewy interior.

- **Toaster:** Quick and classic.
- **Skillet:** Pan-toasting bread in a skillet with a little butter or olive oil makes it nice and golden brown, with the perfect crunch.
- **Broiler:** Perfect for multi-step toasts, when the toppings also need heating.
- **Toaster oven:** Versatile and great for finishing toasts with toppings like melty cheese.

 STEP 3 ## PICK A BASE

Every great toast needs a creamy or spreadable layer to serve as the foundation. This is when you start to build layers of flavor.

Savory Toast Bases

- **Confit:** Garlic Confit (page 310) or Tomato Confit (page 312)
- **Avocado:** Lends a creamy texture in all its forms. Best when mashed and spread on the toast, or sliced and fanned out.

- **Creamy cheese:** Cream cheese, cottage cheese, goat cheese, ricotta, feta. Rich and tangy, they pair perfectly with a variety of proteins and vegetables.

- **Hummus or bean spreads:** Savory and earthy

- **Bacon jam:** The perfect combination of sweet and savory

Sweet Toast Bases

- **Nut butters:** Creamy, slightly salty

- **Cheese:** Mascarpone, ricotta, brie, Gruyère—anything that pairs well with fruits and other sweets

- **Yogurt:** For a light, tangy base

- **Spiced butter:** Softened butter mixed with cinnamon sugar, apple cinnamon sugar, or even pumpkin spice

- **Apple butter:** Sweet with a hint of warm spices

STEP 4 PILE ON THE TOPPINGS

Now you can get really creative. Pile on as many toppings as you see fit. Don't be afraid to try new and different flavor profiles. Many of my toast creations were the result of trying to use up random ingredients before going grocery shopping.

Savory Toast Toppings

- **Protein:** Fried, poached, or jammy hard-boiled eggs, smoked salmon, prosciutto, crispy bacon, Black Forest ham, sausage, roasted chicken

- **Vegetables** (fresh, roasted, or pickled): Tomatoes, caramelized onions, peppers, pickled red onions, kimchi, fresh greens

- **Cheese** (crumbled or shredded): Feta, goat cheese, blue cheese, sharp cheddar, mozzarella, Gruyère, Parmesan, creamy burrata

- **Crunch:** Toasted nuts, seeds, crispy bacon, crushed croutons, Crispy Garlic Chickpeas (page 84), toasted breadcrumbs for textural contrast.

Sweet Toast Toppings

- **Fruits** (fresh, roasted, or stewed): Berries, figs, peaches, bananas, pears, apples

- **Compotes and jams:** Jam, preserves, or slow-cooked fruit compote for extra depth

- **Crunch:** Granola, toasted coconut flakes, chopped pistachios

STEP

5 FINISH WITH GARNISHES

Garnishing may just be my favorite step. It's when you get to add the final pops of color and flavor. It's when the overall composition and presentation is completed. And it's when you get to make it almost too pretty to eat.

- **Fresh herbs:** Chopped fresh basil, dill, chives, thyme, mint

- **Greens:** Fresh microgreens for added crunch and earthiness; arugula for a nice peppery finish

- **Fruits and vegetables:** Chopped red onion, capers, berries

- **Flaky sea salt:** The perfect finishing touch for both sweet and savory toasts alike

- **Spices:** Red pepper flakes, smoked paprika, or cinnamon for an aromatic lift

- **Sauces and drizzles:** Hot honey, chili crisp, pesto, balsamic glaze, olive oil, syrup, Caper-Dill Hollandaise (page 303), Caesar Dressing (page 305)

- **Lemon zest:** To brighten up both sweet and savory toasts

CHERRY RICOTTA TOAST

SERVES: **2**

PREP TIME: **5 MINUTES**

COOK TIME: **10 MINUTES**

This toast delivers the perfect balance of creamy, tangy, and sweet. A whipped ricotta and cottage cheese spread, brightened with lemon and a touch of spice, pairs beautifully with intense cherry jam. My favorite jam to use in this recipe is Intense Cherry by Bonne Maman.

2 tablespoons olive oil

2 large slices sourdough bread

¼ cup whole-milk ricotta cheese

¼ cup cottage cheese

¼ teaspoon red pepper flakes

½ teaspoon fresh thyme leaves, plus extra for garnish

¼ teaspoon black pepper

½ teaspoon grated lemon zest, plus extra for garnish

1 teaspoon fresh lemon juice

⅓ cup cherry jam with whole cherries

1. Heat a large skillet over medium heat. Drizzle the olive oil evenly over both sides of the bread. Place the slices in the pan and toast for 2 to 3 minutes per side, until golden and crispy.

2. In a food processor, blend the ricotta, cottage cheese, red pepper flakes, thyme, black pepper, and lemon zest and juice until smooth and creamy.

3. Spread the whipped ricotta mixture generously onto each slice of toast, making sure to go edge-to-edge for full coverage. Spoon the cherry jam on top of the ricotta and garnish with thyme leaves and lemon zest.

BENEDICT TOAST with CARAMELIZED ONIONS

SERVES: **2**

PREP TIME: **10 MINUTES**

COOK TIME: **30 MINUTES**

This twist on the classic eggs Benedict brings together sweet caramelized onions, savory Black Forest ham, and a perfectly cooked sunny-side-up egg on a crispy, golden sourdough base, topped with rich, velvety hollandaise and fresh herbs.

2 tablespoons olive oil

2 large slices sourdough bread

2 tablespoons salted butter

1 medium sweet onion, thinly sliced

1 ripe avocado, peeled, pitted, and thinly sliced

6 slices Black Forest ham

2 large eggs

Herby Everything Seasoning (page 314)

¼ cup hollandaise sauce (see Tips & Notes in Caper-Dill Hollandaise recipe, page 303)

2 tablespoons chopped fresh chives

Red pepper flakes, for garnish

1. Preheat a large skillet over medium heat. Drizzle the olive oil evenly over both sides of the bread. Place the slices in the pan and toast for 2 to 3 minutes per side, until golden and crispy. Remove from the skillet and keep warm.

2. In the same skillet, cook the onion in the butter over medium-low heat, stirring occasionally, until the onion is soft and caramelized, about 20 minutes.

3. Fan out half of the avocado onto each slice of toast. Layer the caramelized onion and then the ham onto each piece of toast.

4. Crack the eggs into the same skillet. Sprinkle with everything seasoning and cook until the whites are set but the yolks are still runny, 3 to 4 minutes.

5. Lay one egg on top of each toast. Drizzle with the hollandaise and garnish with the chives and red pepper flakes.

GREEN EGGS and HAM ON TOAST

SERVES: **2**

PREP TIME: **5 MINUTES**

COOK TIME: **15 MINUTES**

Pan-toasted sourdough topped with roasted garlic, herby pesto, salty Black Forest ham, and creamy feta forms the ultimate base for perfectly cooked eggs, nestled directly in the sizzling pesto mixture. It's simple, but packed with bold flavors, and feels like something you'd order at your favorite brunch spot.

2 tablespoons olive oil

2 large slices sourdough bread

4 cloves Garlic Confit (page 310) or Whole Roasted Garlic (page 311)

¼ cup pesto, divided

4 thin slices Black Forest ham, cut into strips

4 tablespoons crumbled feta cheese, divided, plus extra for garnish

4 large eggs, divided

2 tablespoons freshly grated Parmesan cheese, for garnish

Red pepper flakes, for garnish

1. Preheat a large skillet over medium heat. Drizzle the olive oil over both sides of the bread. Place the slices in the pan and toast for 2 to 3 minutes per side, until golden and crispy. Spread two roasted garlic cloves on each piece of toast. Lower the heat to medium-low.

2. In the same skillet, spread 2 tablespoons of the pesto into an even round. Scatter half of the ham and 2 tablespoons of the crumbled feta into the pesto, letting it sizzle for 30 seconds.

3. Crack two eggs directly on top of the pesto mixture. Cover the skillet with a lid and cook until the whites are set but the yolks are still runny, 3 to 4 minutes. Carefully slide the eggs, pesto, ham, and feta mixture onto one slice of toast.

4. Repeat steps 2 and 3 for the second toast. Garnish the toasts with more feta, the Parmesan cheese, and red pepper flakes.

PIZZA EGGS on TOAST

This toast takes everything you love about pizza—savory sauce, melty mozzarella, crispy pepperoni—and pairs it with perfectly cooked eggs on golden sourdough. With a touch of garlic confit and finish of Parmesan, red pepper flakes, and parsley, it's the perfect fork-and-knife brunch dish.

4 tablespoons olive oil, divided

2 large slices sourdough bread

4 cloves Garlic Confit (page 310) or Whole Roasted Garlic (page 311)

4 large eggs, divided

¼ cup pizza sauce, divided

¼ cup mini pepperoni slices, divided

¼ cup shredded mozzarella cheese, divided

FOR GARNISH

2 tablespoons freshly grated Parmesan cheese

1 tablespoon chopped fresh flat-leaf parsley

Red pepper flakes

1. Preheat a large skillet over medium heat. Drizzle 2 tablespoons of the olive oil evenly over both sides of the bread. Place the slices in the pan and toast for 2 to 3 minutes per side, until golden and crispy. Spread 2 cloves of garlic confit on each slice of toast.

2. In the same skillet, heat 1 tablespoon of olive oil over medium-low heat. Crack two eggs into the pan. As the eggs are cooking, drop half of the pizza sauce in dollops over the tops to let it cook into the eggs. Sprinkle half of the pepperoni and half of the mozzarella over the top, letting it melt into the whites as they cook. Cover the skillet and cook until the whites are fully set but the yolks are still runny, 3 to 4 minutes. Carefully slide the pizza eggs onto one slice of toast.

3. Repeat step 2 for the second toast. Garnish each toast with the Parmesan, chopped parsley, and a pinch of red pepper flakes.

CAESAR SALAD BREAKFAST TOAST

SERVES: **2**

PREP TIME: **5 MINUTES**

COOK TIME: **20 MINUTES**

2 tablespoons olive oil

2 large slices sourdough bread

4 cloves Garlic Confit (page 310) or Whole Roasted Garlic (page 311)

¼ cup hummus

1 cup chopped romaine lettuce

4 tablespoons Caesar Dressing (page 305), divided

2 hard-boiled eggs

2 tablespoons freshly grated Parmesan cheese, divided

Cracked black pepper, for garnish

2 tablespoons crushed croutons

1. Preheat a large skillet over medium heat. Drizzle the olive oil evenly over both sides of the bread. Place the slices in the pan and toast for 2 to 3 minutes per side, until golden and crispy.

2. Spread 2 cloves of garlic confit onto each slice of toast, then spread the hummus on top.

3. In a bowl, toss the romaine with 3 tablespoons of the dressing. Layer the salad on top of the hummus.

4. Grate a hard-boiled egg over the top of each piece of toast. Top each piece with 1 tablespoon of Parmesan, a drizzle of the remaining dressing, cracked black pepper, and the crushed croutons.

TIPS & NOTES

- **To hard-boil eggs:** *Place the eggs in a saucepan and cover with cold water by about an inch. Bring to a boil over medium-high heat. Once boiling, cover the pot, remove from the heat, and let sit for 9 to 12 minutes, depending on your preferred level of firmness. Transfer the eggs to an ice bath for 5 minutes to cool, then peel.*

DILL EGG SALAD TOAST

A twist on the classic egg salad, this toast features creamy dill egg salad piled high on golden, crispy sourdough. With fresh herbs and nutty Parmesan, it's perfect for breakfast, lunch, or dinner.

2 tablespoons olive oil

2 large slices sourdough bread

4 cloves Garlic Confit (page 310) or Whole Roasted Garlic (page 311)

1 cup Creamy Dill Egg Salad (page 120)

2 tablespoons freshly grated Parmesan cheese

1 teaspoon chopped fresh chives

1 teaspoon chopped fresh dill

Cracked black pepper, for garnish

1. Preheat a large skillet over medium heat. Drizzle the olive oil evenly over both sides of the bread. Place the slices in the pan and toast for 2 to 3 minutes per side, until golden and crispy.

2. Spread 2 cloves of garlic confit onto each slice of toast. Spoon the egg salad evenly onto each piece of toast.

3. Garnish with the Parmesan, chives, dill, and cracked black pepper.

SMOKED SALMON TOAST

SERVES: **2**

PREP TIME: **5 MINUTES**

COOK TIME: **10 MINUTES**

This toast combines silky smoked salmon, herbed cream cheese, and a perfectly cooked sunny-side-up egg, and is seasoned with herby everything goodness. Finished with briny capers, finely chopped red onion, and a bright squeeze of lemon, it's a vibrant, flavor-packed breakfast.

3 tablespoons olive oil, divided

2 large slices sourdough bread

4 cloves Garlic Confit (page 310) or Whole Roasted Garlic (page 311)

⅓ cup cream cheese, softened

1 teaspoon chopped fresh dill, plus extra for garnish

1 teaspoon chopped flat-leaf fresh parsley

Sea salt and cracked black pepper

2 large eggs

Herby Everything Seasoning (page 314)

6 ounces smoked salmon or lox

2 tablespoons capers, drained

2 tablespoons finely chopped red onion

Squeeze of fresh lemon juice

1. Preheat a large skillet over medium heat. Drizzle 2 tablespoons of the olive oil evenly over both sides of the bread. Place the slices in the pan and toast for 2 to 3 minutes per side, until golden and crispy.

2. In a small bowl, mix together the garlic, cream cheese, dill, parsley, a pinch of salt, and cracked black pepper to taste. Spread the herbed cream cheese evenly onto each slice of toast.

3. Using the same skillet, lower the heat to medium-low and add the remaining tablespoon of olive oil. Crack the eggs into the pan and season with the herby everything seasoning. Cook for 3 to 4 minutes, until the whites are set but the yolks are still runny, 3 to 4 minutes.

4. Top each toast with slices of smoked salmon. Carefully slide one egg onto each slice. Garnish with the capers, onion, lemon juice, and additional dill.

CHILI CRISP AVOCADO TOAST

2 tablespoons olive oil

2 large slices sourdough bread

4 cloves Garlic Confit (page 310) or Whole Roasted Garlic (page 311)

1 ripe avocado, peeled, pitted, and mashed

½ cup cottage cheese, divided

2 soft-boiled eggs, peeled

1 tablespoon chili crisp

2 teaspoons hot honey

2 green onions, thinly sliced

1. Preheat a large skillet over medium heat. Drizzle the olive oil evenly over both sides of the bread. Place the slices in the pan and toast for 2 to 3 minutes per side, until golden and crispy.

2. Spread 2 cloves of garlic confit onto each slice of toast. Spread half of the mashed avocado onto each slice. Divide the cottage cheese evenly between the pieces.

3. Carefully slice the soft-boiled eggs in half lengthwise and place two halves on each toast, yolk side up. Top the toasts with the chili crisp, a drizzle of hot honey, and the green onions.

TIPS & NOTES

- *To make jammy soft-boiled eggs, bring a pot of water to a boil, then reduce to a simmer. Carefully lower the eggs into the water and set a timer for 6 minutes. After the time is up, transfer the eggs to an ice water bath or run them under cold water for 1 to 2 minutes to stop the cooking. Starting from the wider end, gently crack and peel the eggs, then cut them in half to reveal the perfect jammy yolks.*

BLACK FOREST HAM and FETA AVOCADO TOAST

SERVES: **2**

PREP TIME: **5 MINUTES**

COOK TIME: **10 MINUTES**

With every bite of this toast, you get something special: creamy avocado, savory ham, a perfectly cooked egg, and a tangy, salty finish of feta cheese and balsamic glaze. It's the kind of breakfast that looks impressive but comes together in minutes—your new go-to for mornings that call for something a little extra.

3 tablespoons olive oil, divided

2 large slices sourdough bread

4 cloves Garlic Confit (page 310) or Whole Roasted Garlic (page 311)

1 ripe avocado, peeled, pitted, and thinly sliced

6 slices Black Forest ham

2 large eggs

1 teaspoon Herby Everything Seasoning (page 314)

3 tablespoons crumbled feta cheese

2 tablespoons balsamic glaze

2 green onions, thinly sliced

1. Preheat a large skillet over medium heat. Drizzle 2 tablespoons of the olive oil evenly over both sides of the bread. Place the slices in the pan and toast for 2 to 3 minutes per side, until golden and crispy.

2. Spread 2 cloves of garlic confit onto each slice of toast. Fan out half of the sliced avocado on each piece of toast. Fold three slices of ham onto each toast, layering them to add height and texture.

3. Using the same skillet, lower the heat to medium-low and add the remaining tablespoon of olive oil. Crack the eggs into the pan and season with the everything seasoning. Cover the skillet and cook until the whites are set but the yolks are still runny, 3 to 4 minutes.

4. Carefully place one egg on top of each piece of toast. Sprinkle with the feta cheese, drizzle with the balsamic glaze, and top with the sliced green onions.

TOMATO CONFIT TOAST

SERVES: **2**

PREP TIME: **5 MINUTES**

COOK TIME: **10 MINUTES**

This toast is a layered masterpiece of creamy ricotta, luscious tomato confit, and earthy roasted garlic that is topped with a perfectly runny egg and seasoned to perfection. Drizzled with balsamic glaze and brightened with fresh basil, every bite balances rich, herby, and tangy flavors—fancy enough for brunch but easy enough for busy weekday mornings.

3 tablespoons olive oil, divided

2 large slices sourdough bread

4 cloves Garlic Confit (page 310) or Whole Roasted Garlic (page 311)

½ cup whole-milk ricotta cheese

1 cup Tomato Confit (page 312)

2 tablespoons pesto

2 large eggs

1 teaspoon Herby Everything Seasoning (page 314)

1 tablespoon balsamic glaze

5 fresh basil leaves, chiffonade

Flaky sea salt, for garnish

1. Preheat a large skillet over medium heat. Drizzle 2 tablespoons of the olive oil evenly over both sides of the bread. Place the slices in the pan and toast for 2 to 3 minutes per side, until golden and crispy.

2. Spread 2 cloves of garlic confit on each slice of toast. Follow with a generous layer of ricotta cheese, spreading evenly to the edges. Spoon the tomato confit over the slices of toast and drizzle the pesto across the tops.

3. In the same skillet, heat the remaining tablespoon of olive oil over medium heat. Crack the eggs into the pan, cover, and cook until the whites are set but the yolks are still runny, 3 to 4 minutes. Sprinkle the everything seasoning generously over the eggs as they cook.

4. Place one egg on each prepared slice of toast. Drizzle with the balsamic glaze, sprinkle with the basil chiffonade, and finish with a pinch of flaky salt.

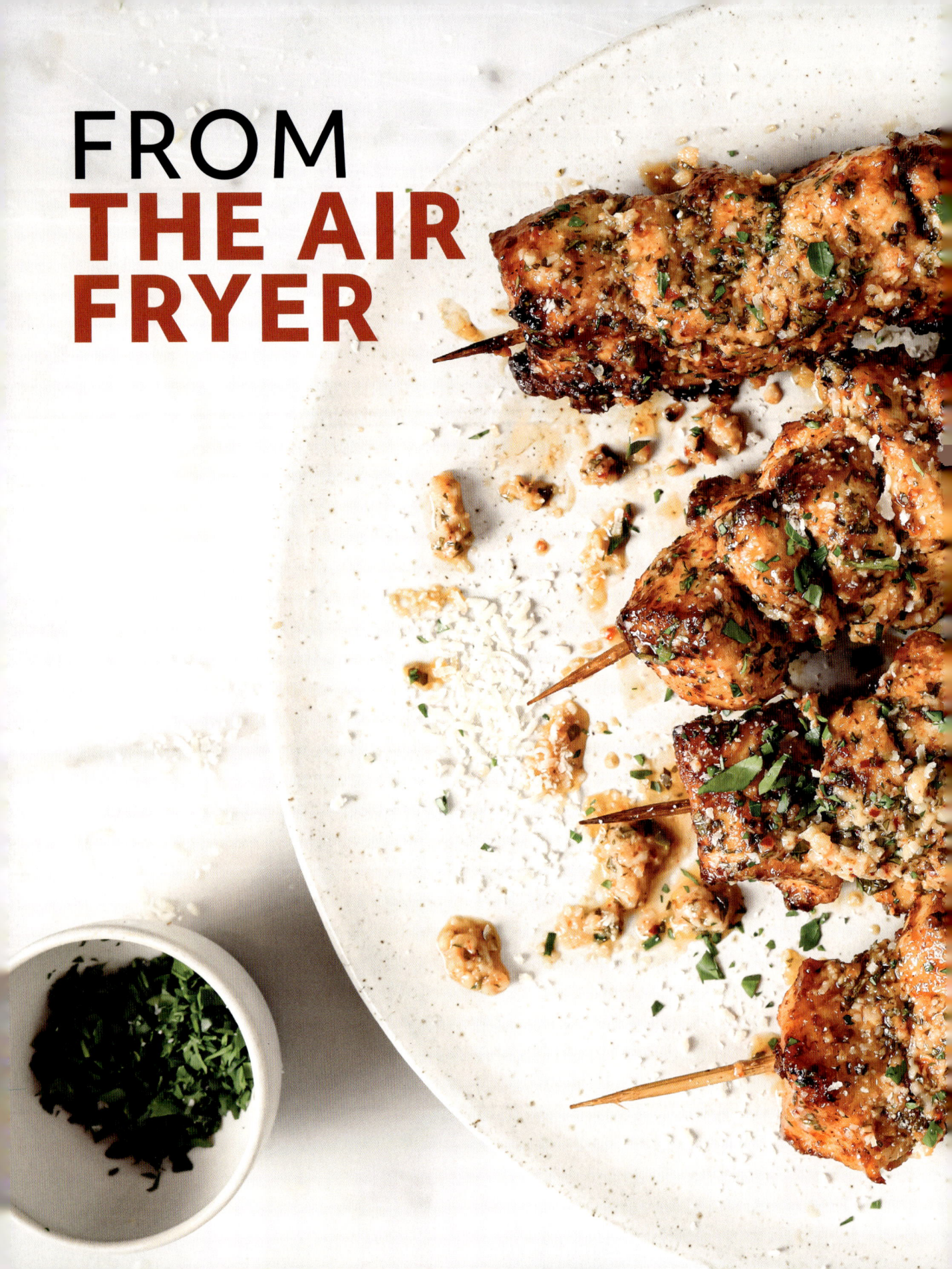

FROM
THE AIR
FRYER

If you've ever found yourself wondering whether yet another appliance is worth the hype (or the counter space), let me assure you that the air fryer definitely is. Compact, versatile, and shockingly efficient, the air fryer takes your favorite cooking methods like baking, roasting, frying, and even toasting and makes them even quicker and easier.

If you're shopping for a new air fryer, I highly recommend going with a toaster oven–style air fryer with an aluminum tray and basket versus the upright version with a plastic basket. The toaster oven style cooks more evenly and efficiently and is a lot safer to use since you are not repeatedly heating and cooking in plastic.

HOW AIR FRYERS WORK

An air fryer is, at its core, a mini convection oven. It uses a heating element and a high-powered fan to circulate hot air around food. This rapid circulation mimics the effect of deep-frying by creating a crispy exterior while keeping the interior of the food tender. What's even better is that you can achieve these results with only a fraction of the oil you'd use in traditional frying methods.

WHAT ABOUT THE CONVECTION FEATURE OF A CONVENTIONAL OVEN?

For those who don't want to invest in another countertop kitchen appliance, many newer conventional ovens have a convection setting. While a dedicated air fryer will be faster, and possibly more efficient due to its size, using the convection setting on your oven will have the same effect. Here's what the convection setting in an oven means:

- **Fan activation:** When convection baking, the fan and exhaust system inside the oven turn on, circulating hot air around the food.

- **Faster cooking:** Since convection ovens cook food faster, using the convection setting of an oven requires lower temperatures and shorter cooking times. For example, what might take 1 hour in a conventional oven could take 45 to 50 minutes in convection mode.

- **Even cooking:** The convection setting ensures that heat is evenly distributed, so multiple dishes or items can cook consistently. This is particularly useful when you're baking on multiple racks at the same time or when roasting large cuts of meat.

OVEN-TO-AIR FRYER CONVERSION CHART

Here's a quick reference guide for converting oven temperatures and times to air fryer settings, in case you'd like to make a recipe written for the oven in your air fryer instead. (Note that the recipes in this chapter are all written for the air fryer, so no adjustments are needed!)

Oven Temp	Air Fryer Temp	Oven Time	Air Fryer Time
400°F	375°F	20 minutes	14 to 16 minutes
375°F	350°F	25 minutes	18 to 20 minutes
350°F	325°F	30 minutes	22 to 25 minutes
325°F	300°F	35 minutes	25 to 28 minutes

Adjust these times and temperatures based on the food type and your specific air fryer model.

AIR FRYER COOKING METHODS

The air fryer excels at a wide variety of cooking techniques. Here are the main methods to master:

- **Frying:** With just a light coating of oil or cooking spray, the air fryer replicates the crispiness of deep frying. Frozen favorites like fries, onion rings, and mozzarella sticks are naturals, but homemade options like breaded chicken or tempura vegetables are where the air fryer really shines.

- **Roasting:** Vegetables like Brussels sprouts, potatoes, carrots, and cauliflower roast in the air fryer in half the time of a conventional oven. Meats like chicken thighs, salmon fillets, and even pork tenderloin stay juicy with caramelized, crispy edges.

- **Baking:** Yes, you can bake in an air fryer. Small-batch cookies, brownies, or muffins come together quickly with crisp edges and soft centers. It's ideal when you don't want to heat up your entire oven for a few sweet treats.

- **Reheating:** Skip the soggy leftovers. The air fryer is unbeatable for reviving foods like pizza, fried chicken, and roasted potatoes, restoring their crispy glory in minutes without drying them out.

- **Toasting:** Use the air fryer to toast nuts, breadcrumbs, or even a slice of sourdough with far more even browning than a traditional toaster or toaster oven.

HOW TO AIR-FRY LIKE A PRO

The air fryer is designed to make cooking faster, easier, and cleaner, but a few simple tips and tricks will ensure perfectly cooked food every time.

- **Avoid overcrowding:** To achieve that perfectly crispy finish, your food needs space for air to circulate. Arrange items in a single layer; don't pile them on top of each other. Overcrowding will cause food to steam instead of crisping up. For larger portions, cook in multiple batches.

- **Preheat:** While many air fryer instructions claim that preheating isn't required, I've found that preheating for 3 to 5 minutes ensures even cooking and better browning, especially for proteins and roasted vegetables.

- **Shake or flip:** For small items like fries, vegetables, or nuggets, shaking the basket or tray halfway through the cooking time ensures everything cooks evenly.

- **Use oil sparingly, but strategically:** Use an oil mister or cooking spray to coat food lightly. Stick to high-smoke-point oils like avocado oil for best results when air-frying above 350°F.

- **Line wisely:** While parchment paper and aluminum foil can make cleanup easier, don't cover the entire tray or basket. Restricting airflow undermines the entire purpose of an air fryer. This is another reason I recommend going with a toaster oven–style air fryer, as it has a tray and a basket. You can line the tray for easy cleanup without restricting airflow from circulating all the way around the food in the basket.

- **Clean as you go:** To prevent lingering odors and ensure your air fryer works efficiently, clean the basket and tray after every use. For sticky messes, soak the basket and tray in warm, soapy water for a few minutes before scrubbing.

 A NOTE ON SAFETY

While air fryers are incredibly easy to use, they get hot—fast. Always use oven mitts when removing the basket or tray. Never place an air fryer on a heat-sensitive surface, and be sure there's enough clearance around the appliance for proper ventilation (that is, not too close to the wall or other appliances).

SALMON and CILANTRO-LIME SLAW

SERVES: **4**

PREP TIME: **20 MINUTES**

COOK TIME: **10 MINUTES**

FOR THE SALMON

4 (6-ounce) salmon fillets

2 tablespoons olive oil

1 teaspoon garlic powder

Sea salt and black pepper

FOR THE SLAW

2½ cups shredded green cabbage

2½ cups shredded red cabbage

1 medium carrot, shredded

⅓ cup sliced green onions

2 tablespoons chopped fresh cilantro, plus extra for garnish

FOR THE DRESSING

½ cup mayonnaise

3 tablespoons olive oil

1½ tablespoons fresh lime juice

2 teaspoons apple cider vinegar

½ teaspoon garlic powder

½ teaspoon sea salt

¼ teaspoon black pepper

½ teaspoon sugar or maple syrup (optional)

1. Preheat the air fryer to 400°F for 5 minutes.

2. Use a paper towel to pat the salmon dry. Brush both sides with the olive oil and season generously with the garlic powder, salt, and pepper. Arrange the fillets in a single layer across the tray or basket of your air fryer. Air-fry for 8 to 10 minutes, until the fish is soft, flaky, and cooked through.

3. Meanwhile, make the slaw: Toss the cabbages, carrot, green onions, and cilantro in a large mixing bowl to combine.

4. Put all of the dressing ingredients in a food processor or high-powered blender and pulse until smooth. Taste and add more salt and pepper, if desired. Mix half of the dressing into the slaw.

5. Plate each piece of salmon with a side of slaw, drizzle a little more dressing over the top, and garnish with additional cilantro. Serve the remaining dressing on the side.

TIPS & NOTES

- *Salmon Selection: I recommend using wild-caught salmon, as it has a firmer texture and deeper flavor. If your fillets are very thick, you might need to add a minute or two to the cook time.*

- *No Air Fryer? No Problem! You can roast the salmon in a 400°F oven for 12 to 14 minutes, or pan-sear it in a skillet over medium-high heat until just cooked through.*

- *Slaw Shortcuts: In a hurry? Grab a preshredded coleslaw mix from the grocery store. Just toss it with the dressing and you're good to go.*

TUNA MELT FRITTERS

2 (5-ounce) cans albacore tuna, drained

½ cup panko breadcrumbs

½ cup shredded sharp white cheddar cheese

¼ cup shredded mozzarella cheese

¼ cup mayonnaise

¼ cup finely chopped celery

¼ cup finely chopped red onion

1 large egg

2 tablespoons chopped fresh dill, plus extra for garnish

1 tablespoon Dijon mustard

2 teaspoons Worcestershire sauce

½ teaspoon garlic powder

½ teaspoon onion powder

¼ teaspoon smoked paprika

Sea salt and black pepper, to taste

FOR SERVING

Lemon wedges

Yum Yum Sauce (page 306)

1. Put all of the ingredients for the fritters in a large mixing bowl and mix until well incorporated. Using your hands, form the mixture into 12 small fritters, 2 to 3 inches in diameter and about ½ inch thick.

2. Preheat the air fryer to 375°F for 5 minutes.

3. Lightly spray the air fryer tray or basket with avocado oil cooking spray. Arrange the fritters in a single layer, making sure they do not overlap; you may need to cook them in batches. Lightly spray the tops of the fritters with cooking spray for extra crispiness.

4. Air-fry the fritters for 8 to 10 minutes, flipping them halfway through and spraying the other side with cooking spray. When done, they should be golden brown and crispy on both sides.

5. Garnish with additional dill and serve with lemon wedges and yum yum sauce.

TIPS & NOTES

- *I love a good crispy, gooey, diner-style tuna melt. That was my inspiration for this recipe.*

- *The fritters can also be made with canned salmon or even canned chicken.*

- *For low-carb and gluten-free fritters, swap out the panko for crushed pork rinds.*

GARLIC PARMESAN CHICKEN SKEWERS

SERVES: **4**

PREP TIME: **15 MINUTES**

COOK TIME: **15 MINUTES**

FOR THE CHICKEN

2 pounds boneless, skinless chicken thighs, cut into large chunks

2 tablespoons olive oil

2 teaspoons smoked paprika

1½ teaspoons onion powder

1 teaspoon garlic powder

1 teaspoon sea salt

½ teaspoon black pepper

FOR THE HERBED BUTTER

½ cup (1 stick) salted butter, melted

8 cloves garlic, minced

½ cup finely grated Parmesan cheese, plus extra for garnish

¼ cup minced fresh flat-leaf parsley, plus extra for garnish

1 teaspoon grated lemon zest

2 tablespoons fresh lemon juice

1 teaspoon hot sauce

1 teaspoon red pepper flakes

1. In a large mixing bowl, drizzle the chicken chunks with the olive oil and toss until evenly coated. Mix the paprika, onion powder, garlic powder, salt, and pepper in a small bowl, then pour the seasoning mixture over the chicken and toss until evenly coated.

2. Divide the chicken evenly among six skewers, tightly packing it onto each skewer and leaving no gaps to ensure it stays nice and juicy.

3. Preheat the air fryer to 400°F for 5 minutes.

4. Make the herbed butter: In a medium bowl, combine all of the ingredients for the herbed butter. Set aside one-third of it in a separate bowl to baste the cooked chicken.

5. Depending on the size and style of your air fryer, you may need to cook the chicken skewers in two batches. Air-fry the skewers for 5 minutes. Flip the skewers and baste generously with the herbed butter. Air-fry for another 3 minutes. Flip the skewers again and baste the other side generously with the herbed butter. Cook for 5 minutes more, until the chicken reaches an internal temperature of 165°F.

6. With a clean basting brush, baste the skewers one final time with the reserved herbed butter. Garnish the skewers with a little Parmesan and fresh parsley before serving.

TIPS & NOTES

- *No air fryer? No problem! These skewers can be grilled over medium-high heat for 10 to 12 minutes, flipping and basting as directed. They can also be baked at 425°F for 20 to 25 minutes, flipping and basting halfway through.*

- *If using wooden skewers, soak them in water for at least 30 minutes to prevent burning.*

- *For a seafood twist, swap the chicken for large shrimp and reduce the cooking time to 6 to 8 minutes total.*

SPICE-RUBBED PORK TENDERLOIN

2 (1-pound) pork tenderloins

3 tablespoons Dijon mustard

3 tablespoons brown sugar

1 tablespoon plus 1 teaspoon smoked paprika

2 teaspoons sea salt

1 teaspoon garlic powder

1 teaspoon onion powder

¾ teaspoon black pepper

1. Preheat the air fryer to 400°F for 5 minutes.

2. Trim the pork tenderloins of any excess fat and silverskin. Coat the tenderloins with the mustard. In a small bowl, combine the brown sugar, paprika, salt, garlic powder, onion powder, and pepper. Rub the spice mixture over the tenderloins, pressing it gently into the mustard so it sticks.

3. Place the pork tenderloins in the air fryer basket or tray. Air-fry for 20 minutes, or until the pork has reached an internal temperature of 145°F.

4. Transfer the tenderloins to a cutting board and let rest for at least 5 minutes before slicing into medallions. Save any juices from the cutting board to serve over the meat.

> **TIPS & NOTES**
>
> - *Alternative Cooking Methods:*
>   - *Roast in the oven at 425°F for 20 to 25 minutes, flipping halfway through.*
>   - *Grill over medium-high heat for 15 to 20 minutes, turning every 5 minutes.*
>   - *Sear in a hot oven-proof skillet for 2 to 3 minutes per side, then transfer to a 400°F oven to finish cooking for 10 to 12 minutes.*
>
> - *The tenderloins are delicious served with Umami Brussels Sprouts (page 259) and Garlic-Herb Mashed Potatoes (page 189).*

UMAMI BRUSSELS SPROUTS

1 pound Brussels sprouts, halved (or quartered if large)

2 tablespoons avocado oil

1 tablespoon umami powder, or more to taste

½ teaspoon garlic powder

½ teaspoon onion powder

¼ teaspoon black pepper

1. Preheat the air fryer to 400°F for 5 minutes.

2. In a large mixing bowl, toss all of the ingredients until the Brussels sprouts are evenly coated in the oil and seasonings.

3. Arrange the sprouts in a single layer in the air fryer basket or tray and cook for 15 to 20 minutes, until they are crisp-tender with charred edges. You may need to cook them in two batches to make sure they are not overcrowded.

TIPS & NOTES

Your tongue has five different taste receptors— bitter, sour sweet, salty, and umami. Umami powder is one of my favorite ways to add that particular savory flavor to food, especially vegetables. Several companies make it now, but my favorite brand is Takii, which is made from shiitake mushrooms and can be found on Amazon.

FURIKAKE POTATO WEDGES

SERVES: **4**

PREP TIME: **10 MINUTES, PLUS 1 HOUR TO SOAK**

COOK TIME: **17 MINUTES**

4 medium russet potatoes

2 tablespoons avocado oil

1½ teaspoons garlic powder

1½ teaspoons onion powder

¾ teaspoon smoked paprika

½ teaspoon black pepper

2 tablespoons furikake, for garnish

Yum Yum Sauce (page 306), for serving

1. Scrub the potatoes and then slice into wedges. Soak the wedges in a bowl of water for 30 minutes to 1 hour. This gets rid of excess starch and helps the potatoes crisp up when air-fried. Drain and dry thoroughly with paper towels.

2. Preheat the air fryer to 400°F for 5 minutes.

3. Put the potato wedges in a large bowl, drizzle the avocado oil over them, and toss until all of the wedges are evenly coated. In a small bowl, combine the garlic powder, onion powder, paprika, and pepper. Sprinkle the spice mixture over the potatoes and toss until evenly coated.

4. Place a single layer of potato wedges in the basket or tray of your air fryer. Air-fry for 10 to 12 minutes, then flip the wedges. Air-fry for another 5 minutes, or until cooked through and crispy. You may need to cook them in batches so they are not overcrowded to get them extra crispy.

5. Garnish with the furikake and serve with yum yum sauce.

TIPS & NOTES

- *You can make your own furikake by combining toasted sesame seeds, nori (dried seaweed), and a touch of salt.*

- *These potatoes are also delicious with bonito flakes on top.*

- *In addition to yum yum sauce, the wedges are excellent with unagi sauce.*

LOADED GREEK FRIES

2 medium russet potatoes (about 1½ pounds), scrubbed

¾ teaspoon sea salt

½ teaspoon dried dill

½ teaspoon dried mint

½ teaspoon dried oregano

½ teaspoon garlic powder

½ teaspoon onion powder

3 tablespoons olive oil, divided

Grated zest of 1 lemon

2 teaspoons chopped fresh dill, plus extra for garnish

2 teaspoons chopped fresh parsley, plus extra for garnish

⅓ cup crumbled feta cheese

¼ cup finely chopped red onion

¼ cup thinly sliced pepperoncini

Cracked black pepper

Cucumber Sauce (page 307), for serving

1. Slice the potatoes into ¼- to ½-inch-thick sticks. Place the sticks in a bowl of water and soak for 30 minutes to 1 hour. This helps remove excess starch and allows the fries to get nice and crispy. Drain and dry thoroughly with paper towels. The drier you get the potatoes, the crispier the fries will be.

2. Preheat the air fryer to 400°F for 5 minutes.

3. In a small bowl, combine the salt, dried herbs, garlic powder, and onion powder. Place the fries in a large mixing bowl, drizzle with 2 tablespoons of the olive oil, and toss to coat. Sprinkle the seasoning mixture over the fries and toss until evenly coated in the oil and seasonings.

4. Spread the fries in a single layer in the air fryer basket or tray. You may need to air-fry in batches to avoid overcrowding. Air-fry for 15 minutes, flipping halfway, until crispy.

5. If you cooked in batches, return all of the fries to the air fryer to warm them through for 1 to 2 minutes. This does not need to be done in a single layer.

6. Transfer the fries to a bowl and toss with the remaining tablespoon of olive oil, the lemon zest, fresh dill, and parsley. Taste and add more salt, if desired.

7. Transfer the fries to a serving platter and top with the feta, onion, and pepperoncini. Garnish with additional fresh herbs and crack some pepper over the top. Serve with the sauce.

TIPS & NOTES

- *Try sweet potatoes for a sweeter, slightly softer fry (reduce the temperature to 375°F and air-fry for 18 to 20 minutes).*

- *For a citrusy punch, squeeze fresh lemon juice over the fries right before serving.*

- *These fries are delicious served alongside Garlic Parmesan Chicken Skewers (page 255).*

PASTA CHIPS

4 ounces rigatoni pasta

4 ounces bow-tie pasta

1 tablespoon avocado oil

¼ cup finely grated Parmesan cheese

½ teaspoon Italian seasoning

½ teaspoon garlic powder

¼ teaspoon onion powder

¼ teaspoon paprika

¼ teaspoon sea salt

¼ teaspoon black pepper

Marinara sauce, for serving

Ranch dressing, for serving

1. Bring a large pot of salted water to a boil. Cook the pasta according to the package directions until al dente, then drain.

2. Preheat the air fryer to 400°F for 5 minutes.

3. In a large mixing bowl, toss the cooked pasta with the avocado oil, Parmesan, Italian seasoning, garlic powder, onion powder, paprika, salt, and pepper.

4. Air-fry for 12 to 14 minutes, until the pasta is golden brown on the edges and crispy, tossing a few times throughout cooking. You may need to air-fry it in multiple batches to avoid overcrowding. Serve with marinara and ranch.

TIPS & NOTES

- *Go beyond marinara and ranch—try dipping the pasta chips in pesto, garlic aioli, sriracha mayo, Alfredo sauce, or even hummus.*

- *For a dairy-free version, swap out the Parmesan cheese for nutritional yeast.*

APPLE HAND PIES

2 Granny Smith apples, cored, peeled, and diced (about 2 cups)

⅓ cup packed brown sugar

1 teaspoon vanilla extract

1 teaspoon ground cinnamon

1 tablespoon cornstarch

1 package frozen unbaked pie crust (not a baked shell)

1 large egg

1 teaspoon water

Warm caramel sauce, for serving

1. Combine the apples, brown sugar, vanilla, and cinnamon in a small saucepan over medium heat. Cook, stirring occasionally, until the apples have softened, 8 to 10 minutes. Add the cornstarch and bring the mixture back up to a boil. Once the sauce has thickened, remove from the heat and allow to cool.

2. Roll out the pie dough in a thin layer. With a 4-inch round cutter, cut rounds from the dough as close together as possible. Remove the cut rounds, then reroll the remaining dough and repeat the process to make 10 dough rounds.

3. Place some of the apple pie filling on one side of each dough round. Using your finger, wet the edge of the dough with a little water. Fold the dough over the filling and match the edges so you have a half-round. Seal the hand pie by pressing a fork around the edges.

4. In a small bowl, whisk together the egg and water. Brush the egg wash over the tops of the pies. With a sharp knife, cut a few slits in the top of each pie for the steam to escape.

5. Preheat the air fryer to 350°F for 5 minutes.

6. Place 5 pies in the air fryer basket or tray, in one layer and not touching. Air-fry for 8 to 10 minutes, until the crusts are golden brown and the filling is starting to bubble out. Repeat with the remaining pies. Serve with warm caramel sauce for dipping.

> **TIPS & NOTES**
>
> *These hand pies can also be made with chopped peaches, cherries, or mixed berries. Simply replace the apples with 2 cups fruit of your choice.*

BRÛLÉE BANANAS

2 large bananas

¼ cup packed light brown sugar

¼ teaspoon ground cinnamon, plus extra for garnish

2 large scoops vanilla ice cream

3 tablespoons caramel sauce

2 tablespoons crushed pistachios

1. Preheat the air fryer to 400°F for 5 minutes.

2. Peel the bananas and slice in half lengthwise. Place the banana halves in the air fryer tray or basket. Cover the bananas liberally with the brown sugar and then sprinkle with the cinnamon.

3. Place the bananas in the air fryer (if using a tray-style air fryer, place the tray on the top rack). Air-fry for 7 to 10 minutes, until the brown sugar is melted and bubbling. (Start checking around the 7-minute mark to ensure they don't burn.) Remove from the air fryer and let the sugar cool and harden just a bit to create a candy shell on the bananas.

4. Plate each serving with two banana halves, topping with the ice cream, caramel sauce, and pistachios. Garnish with a sprinkle of cinnamon.

TIPS & NOTES

- *Choose ripe but firm bananas: Overripe bananas may become too soft in the air fryer. Look for bananas that have a few brown speckles but are still firm to the touch.*

- *Add a pinch of nutmeg, cardamom, or ginger for a warm spiced flavor.*

- *Twists on the toppings: Add a drizzle of hot fudge or chocolate sauce. Swap out the pistachios for roasted pecans, walnuts, or hazelnuts.*

CASSEROLES
AND
PASTAS

There are few meals as comforting or versatile as a casserole or bowl of pasta. There's something universally welcoming about a bubbling casserole pulled fresh from the oven or a piping hot bowl of perfectly sauced pasta with a mountain of freshly grated cheese.

Casserole and pasta recipes are the ones that get passed down through generations, telling stories of cozy winter nights, bustling family dinners, and how they came to be from creative leftover transformations. But beyond their nostalgic charm, they are some of the most versatile and forgiving recipes you can keep in your cooking rotation.

THE ANATOMY of a GREAT CASSEROLE

Casseroles are about working with what you've got and creating something that feels intentional, even when it's thrown together. That said, there are five basic elements to keep in mind when putting together a casserole.

1. **Base:** Pasta, rice, potatoes, bread, or any other sturdy starch

2. **Protein:** Rotisserie chicken, ground beef, pork, seafood, ham, bacon, or sausage to add heartiness

3. **Vegetables and herbs:** Fresh, frozen, or roasted vegetables to add color, texture, and nutrients; fresh herbs like chives, parsley, oregano, or thyme to add a vibrant, fresh flavor

4. **Sauce:** Béchamel, marinara, Alfredo, pesto, cheese sauce, enchilada sauce, salsa, gravy, egg mixture, seasoned butter, or any other sauce to tie everything together

5. **Topping:** Bubbly cheese, crispy breadcrumbs, crunchy fried onions, and more for the perfect finish and textural contrast

A casserole lends itself to a lot of creative experimentation for both sweet and savory dishes. Start with what you have in your fridge or pantry (pasta, potatoes, etc.) and build from there. Extra chicken from last night's dinner? Perfect. Leftover roasted vegetables? Toss them in. There really are no rules.

THE ANATOMY of GREAT PASTA

A truly great pasta is more than just noodles tossed in sauce. It's also about balancing texture and flavor. These are not exhaustive lists, but rather ideas to get your creative juices flowing:

1. **Pasta:** Start with the right shape to match your sauce.

   - **Long:** Spaghetti, linguine, bucatini, and fettuccine are best with light, silky sauces like aglio e olio, creamy carbonara, and classic marinara; or with heavier sauces like creamy garlic Alfredo.

- **Short:** Penne, rigatoni, and farfalle are perfect for holding onto chunky sauces like Bolognese, creamy vodka sauce, and vibrant pesto.

- **Twisted or ridged shapes:** Fusilli, cavatappi, and rotini are great for grabbing onto thick sauces and bits of cheese, meat, and vegetables.

- **Stuffed pasta:** Ravioli, tortellini, and the like shine with delicate sauces like brown butter, sage, and Tomato Confit (page 312).

2. **Sauce:** The sauce is the star of the show, coating each noodle perfectly.

- **Tomato-based:** Bright and zesty marinara, spicy arrabbiata, vodka sauce

- **Creamy sauces:** Decadent Alfredo, creamy pesto, cheese-based sauces

- **Oil-based:** Garlic and olive oil, chili oil, fresh pesto

- **Meat- or stock-based:** Ragu, beef short rib, or seafood broth with wine and aromatics

Pro Tip: To elevate store-bought pasta sauce and add depth of flavor, add Garlic Confit (page 310), Tomato Confit (page 312), or fresh herbs.

3. **Flavor boosters:** Simple ingredients can add massive flavor.

- **Aromatics:** Sautéed garlic, shallots, roasted onions to complement an acidic or creamy sauce

- **Herbs:** Fresh basil, parsley, oregano, sage for brightness; thyme, rosemary for earthiness

- **Acid:** A squeeze of lemon, splash of vinegar, dash of white wine to elevate the sauce

- **Umami bombs:** Anchovies melted into oil, Parmesan rinds simmered in sauce, a dollop of miso paste

- **Heat:** Chili flakes, cracked pepper, chili crisp for gentle heat

4. **Add-ins:** Make it a hearty, complete meal by adding protein and vegetables.

- **Protein:** Meatballs, Italian sausage, pancetta, prosciutto, shredded chicken, shrimp—the possibilities are endless

- **Vegetables:** Fresh spinach, kale, zucchini ribbons, mushrooms, onions, charred broccoli rabe, oven-roasted tomatoes

- **Cheese:** Ricotta, fresh mozzarella, goat cheese, feta, sharp cheddar, Parmigiano-Reggiano

5. **Finishing touches:** These can make the difference between a great pasta and an unforgettable one.

  - **Crunch:** Homemade breadcrumbs toasted in butter (with Herby Everything Seasoning, page 314), toasted nuts, seeds

  - **Fresh herbs:** A final sprinkle of fresh herbs like parsley, basil, or chives for brightness

  - **Cheese:** A generous amount of freshly grated Parmesan or Pecorino Romano

  - **Final boost:** A swirl of good-quality olive oil or truffle oil, Garlic Confit (page 310), crispy prosciutto, crispy sage, a squeeze of lemon juice or zest, chili flakes, cracked black pepper

Pro Tip: Keep cooked proteins, shredded cheese, and prechopped veggies in the fridge or freezer so you're always just minutes away from assembling the perfect casserole or making a restaurant-quality pasta dish.

HOW to PROPERLY COOK PASTA

1. **Salt your water (liberally):** The water you boil your pasta in should taste like the sea. This is your chance to season the pasta itself, so don't skimp on the salt. A tablespoon or two for a large pot of water is a good rule of thumb.

2. **Cook just shy of al dente:** If your pasta is headed into a baked casserole or will simmer in sauce for a few minutes, undercook it slightly. This keeps the noodles from turning mushy and allows them to absorb flavor from the sauce.

3. **Reserve some of your pasta water:** That starchy, salty water is liquid gold. A splash or two can loosen thick sauces, help bind ingredients together, and add a silky finish to most any pasta dish.

4. **Sauce and pasta should marry:** Don't just pour sauce over drained noodles and take it to the table. Instead, finish cooking the pasta directly in the sauce for a minute or two. This helps the flavors meld and coat each noodle evenly.

Casseroles and pasta dishes are meant to be shared and savored. They are the ultimate in crowd-pleasing comfort food. They're a canvas for creativity, where simple ingredients come together to create layers of flavor. Let this chapter be your guide to creating meals that bring people together one bubbling bite or twirl of noodles at a time.

BISCUITS and GRAVY CASSEROLE

SERVES: **4**

PREP TIME: **10 MINUTES**

COOK TIME: **50 MINUTES**

6 tablespoons salted butter, divided

1 pound ground pork sausage

1 small yellow onion, chopped

⅓ cup all-purpose flour

3 cups whole milk

¾ cup shredded cheddar cheese

¾ cup shredded pepper jack cheese

1 teaspoon sea salt

½ teaspoon black pepper

½ teaspoon onion powder

½ teaspoon garlic powder

1 (16-ounce) can refrigerated biscuit dough (8 biscuits total)

Chopped fresh chives, for garnish

1. Preheat the oven to 350°F.

2. Melt 1 tablespoon of the butter in a large ovenproof skillet over medium heat. Add the sausage. Use a wooden spoon to crumble the sausage as it cooks. Once the sausage is no longer pink, add the onion and cook until translucent, about 5 minutes. Use a slotted spoon to transfer the sausage and onion to a bowl. Discard the grease from the pan.

3. Reduce the heat to low and add 4 tablespoons of the butter to the same pan, whisking until melted. Whisk in the flour until smooth, then whisk constantly for 1 minute. Increase the heat to medium and gradually whisk in the milk. Cook, whisking constantly, until the gravy is thickened and bubbling, 5 to 6 minutes.

4. Add both cheeses, the salt, pepper, onion powder, and garlic powder to the pan and whisk until the cheese is melted in and the sauce is smooth. Return the sausage mixture to the pan and mix until the ingredients are well combined.

5. Arrange the biscuits across the top of the gravy. Transfer the skillet to the oven and bake until the biscuits are golden brown, about 30 minutes.

6. Melt the remaining tablespoon of butter and brush over the top of the biscuits. Garnish with chives and serve.

TIPS & NOTES

To make this recipe even quicker, you can use prebaked biscuits or scones: simply place them on top of the gravy and bake until they are warmed through, then brush with the butter.

HAM and CHEESE CROISSANT CASSEROLE

SERVES: **6**

PREP TIME: **15 MINUTES, PLUS 30 MINUTES TO CHILL**

COOK TIME: **50 MINUTES**

Butter, for greasing

5 large eggs

1¾ cups half-and-half

1½ cups shredded Gruyère cheese, divided

1½ cups shredded sharp white cheddar cheese, divided

½ cup sour cream

2 tablespoons Dijon mustard

2 tablespoons dried minced onion

2 tablespoons chopped fresh chives, plus extra for garnish

1 tablespoon fresh thyme leaves, plus extra for garnish

1½ teaspoons sea salt

1 teaspoon garlic powder

½ teaspoon black pepper

10 large stale croissants, each cut into 2 or 3 pieces

10 ounces thinly sliced Black Forest ham, each slice cut in half

2 teaspoons Herby Everything Seasoning (page 314)

1. Generously grease a 9- by 13-inch baking dish with butter.

2. Whisk the eggs in a large mixing bowl. Add the half-and-half, ¾ cup of the Gruyère, ¾ cup of the cheddar, the sour cream, mustard, dried onion, chives, thyme, salt, garlic powder, and pepper. Whisk until the ingredients are well incorporated.

3. Arrange the croissants in the baking dish and pour the egg mixture evenly over the top. Toss the croissants to make sure they are evenly coated in the egg mixture. Refrigerate for 30 minutes.

4. Preheat the oven to 350°F.

5. Tuck the ham between the croissants in the casserole dish. Sprinkle the remaining Gruyère and cheddar over the top. Cover the dish with foil and bake for 30 minutes. Uncover and bake for an additional 15 to 20 minutes, until the croissants are a deep golden brown. Garnish with chives, thyme, and the everything seasoning.

TIPS & NOTES

- *This casserole can be assembled the night before and stored in the fridge until ready to bake. Step 5 is done at the time of baking.*

- *If you can't find Black Forest ham, Canadian bacon is an excellent substitute.*

- *In place of the croissants, you can use brioche buns, similar to the French Toast Casserole (page 281).*

FRENCH TOAST CASSEROLE

SERVES: 6

PREP TIME: **20 MINUTES, PLUS 1 HOUR TO STAND**

COOK TIME: **45 MINUTES**

Unsalted butter, for greasing

6 large eggs

1¾ cups milk

6 tablespoons packed brown sugar, divided

1 tablespoon vanilla bean paste

1½ teaspoons ground cinnamon

½ teaspoon sea salt

¼ teaspoon ground nutmeg

8 stale brioche buns (about 1½ pounds total), cut into 1-inch cubes

3 tablespoons unsalted butter, melted

½ cup chopped pecans

FOR SERVING

Maple syrup

Whipped cream

Hulled and quartered strawberries

1. Preheat the oven to 350°F. Grease a 9- by 13-inch baking dish with butter.

2. In a large mixing bowl, whisk together the eggs, milk, 3 tablespoons of the brown sugar, the vanilla bean paste, cinnamon, salt, and nutmeg. Add the cubed brioche and toss until the bread is evenly coated.

3. Pour the mixture into the prepared baking dish. If making the casserole ahead, cover the dish and refrigerate overnight. Otherwise, let stand at room temperature for 1 hour to allow the bread to soak up the egg mixture.

4. In a small bowl, whisk together the melted butter and the remaining 3 tablespoons of brown sugar. Drizzle the mixture over the top of the casserole and top with the pecans. Cover with foil and bake for 30 minutes. Uncover and bake for an additional 15 minutes, or until the topping is browned and the egg mixture has set. Cover loosely with foil and let sit for 10 minutes before serving. Serve with maple syrup, whipped cream, and strawberries.

TIPS & NOTES

- *This casserole is also delicious made with stale croissants, similar to the Ham and Cheese Croissant Casserole (page 278).*

- *Some other delicious toppings for the baked casserole are peanut butter, Nutella, mixed berry compote, chocolate chips, and granola.*

- *I like to serve the casserole with sausage links, crispy bacon, scrambled eggs, and mimosas to make a complete brunch spread.*

CARAMELIZED ONION and PROSCIUTTO MAC and CHEESE

SERVES: **4**

PREP TIME: **15 MINUTES**

COOK TIME: **30 MINUTES**

14 ounces cellentani pasta

2 tablespoons salted butter, divided

1 tablespoon olive oil

1 large yellow onion, diced

6 ounces thinly sliced prosciutto, cut into thin strips

3 cloves garlic, minced

1 cup heavy cream

1 cup shredded sharp cheddar cheese

1 cup finely grated Parmesan cheese, plus extra for garnish

3 ounces goat cheese

½ teaspoon sea salt

½ teaspoon black pepper

1. Cook the pasta according to the package directions until al dente. Drain, reserving 1 cup of the starchy pasta water.

2. In a large skillet over medium heat, melt 1 tablespoon of the butter with the olive oil. Add the onion and sauté for 5 minutes to soften. Reduce the heat to medium-low and cook, stirring occasionally, until the onion is golden brown and caramelized, about 20 minutes. Remove the onion from the pan and set aside. To the same pan, add the prosciutto and cook over medium heat until crispy. Remove from the pan and set aside.

3. In a large saucepan over medium heat, melt the remaining 1 tablespoon of butter. Add the garlic and sauté for 1 minute, until fragrant. Add the cream and bring to a boil. Reduce to a simmer and add the cheddar, Parmesan, goat cheese, salt, and pepper. Mix until all of the cheeses are melted and the ingredients are well incorporated.

4. Add the cooked pasta to the sauce, along with ½ cup of the reserved pasta water. Toss until the pasta is evenly coated with the sauce, adding more pasta water if needed. Taste and add more salt and pepper, if desired. Mix in half of the crispy prosciutto and half of the onion.

5. Transfer the pasta to a serving dish and top with remaining onion and prosciutto.

TIPS & NOTES

This has been one of my favorite recipes for as long as I can remember. It hearkens back to my low-carb days, as I originally wrote the recipe with cauliflower in place of pasta. To substitute cauliflower, simply steam a whole head of cauliflower in chicken stock, or dry-roast small florets on a sheet pan at 425°F for about 20 minutes, until they are crisp-tender with slightly charred edges.

TUSCAN CHICKEN PASTA

SERVES: **4**

PREP TIME: **15 MINUTES**

COOK TIME: **30 MINUTES**

14 ounces penne pasta

1 pound boneless, skinless chicken breasts or thighs, cubed

1 teaspoon paprika

1 teaspoon onion powder

1 teaspoon sea salt

½ teaspoon black pepper

2 tablespoons olive oil

2 tablespoons salted butter

1 small red onion, thinly sliced

6 cloves garlic, minced

¼ cup dry white wine

¼ cup chicken stock

⅔ cup sun-dried tomatoes, drained if using oil-packed

1½ cups heavy cream

½ cup finely grated Parmesan cheese, plus extra for garnish

3 cups baby spinach leaves

Chopped fresh flat-leaf parsley, for garnish

Red pepper flakes, for garnish

1. Cook the pasta according to the package directions until al dente. Drain and set aside.

2. While the pasta is cooking, season the chicken all over with the paprika, onion powder, salt, and pepper. Heat the olive oil in a large skillet over medium-high heat. Add the chicken and sear on all sides until golden brown, about 8 minutes. Remove the chicken from the pan and set aside.

3. To the same pan, add the butter. Once it has melted, add the onion and sauté until tender, about 8 minutes. Add the garlic and sauté until fragrant, about 1 minute. Deglaze the pan with the white wine and stock, using a rubber spatula to scrape up and mix in any bits that are stuck to the bottom of the pan.

4. Add the sun-dried tomatoes to the pan and cook for 2 to 3 minutes. Add the cream, bring to a slow boil, and reduce the heat to a simmer. Stir in the Parmesan until it is melted into the sauce. Taste and add more salt and pepper, if desired. Add the spinach to the sauce and let cook until it is wilted down and tender.

5. Add the chicken to the sauce along with the drained pasta and toss to combine. Garnish with parsley, red pepper flakes, and additional Parmesan.

TIPS & NOTES

- *Shrimp makes a fantastic swap for chicken—just cook it quickly (2–3 minutes per side) and add it back at the end.*

- *For a vegetarian option, use white beans or chickpeas for protein.*

- *Italian sausage (mild or spicy) brings a rich, savory element.*

- *Good wines to use in this recipe include Sauvignon Blanc, Pinot Grigio, Viognier, and chardonnay. If you do not have wine on hand, or do not wish to cook with wine, you can substitute extra chicken stock.*

MUSHROOM ORZO with CRISPY PROSCIUTTO and SAGE

SERVES: **4**

PREP TIME: **15 MINUTES**

COOK TIME: **30 MINUTES**

8 ounces uncooked orzo

2 tablespoons olive oil

6 slices prosciutto

4 tablespoons salted butter, divided

12 fresh sage leaves

8 ounces shiitake mushrooms, stems removed and caps quartered

8 ounces cremini mushrooms, sliced

1 large shallot, minced

5 cloves garlic, minced

½ teaspoon red pepper flakes

½ cup heavy cream

1 teaspoon sea salt

½ teaspoon black pepper

½ cup freshly grated Parmesan cheese, plus shaved Parmesan for garnish

2 packed cups fresh baby spinach

Grated zest and juice of 1 small lemon

1. Cook the orzo according to the package directions until just a couple minutes shy of al dente. Drain, reserving 1½ cups of the starchy pasta water.

2. Heat the olive oil in a large high-sided skillet over medium heat. Add the prosciutto slices and fry until they are nice and crispy, 2 to 3 minutes per side. As they cook, they will naturally curl into bundles. Transfer to a paper towel–lined plate and set aside.

3. In the same skillet, melt 1 tablespoon of the butter. Add the sage leaves and fry until crispy, 1 to 2 minutes. Transfer to a paper towel–lined plate and let cool. Crush half of the fried sage leaves and leave the remaining whole for garnish.

4. Add 2 more tablespoons of the butter to the skillet and increase the heat to medium-high. Add all of the mushrooms and cook, stirring occasionally, until browned, 7 to 8 minutes. Add the remaining tablespoon of butter, the shallot, garlic, and red pepper flakes and sauté for 2 to 3 minutes, until fragrant. Add the cream, salt, and pepper and stir to combine. Add the drained orzo along with 1 cup of the reserved pasta water and cook over medium heat, stirring frequently until the orzo is al dente and the sauce has thickened to a creamy consistency.

5. Remove the pan from the heat. Stir in the grated Parmesan until melted and creamy. Add the crushed sage, spinach, lemon zest, and lemon juice. Stir gently until the ingredients are well combined and the spinach has wilted. If the dish seems too dry, add more of the reserved pasta water. Taste and add more salt and pepper, if desired.

6. Garnish with the shaved Parmesan cheese, fried sage leaves, and prosciutto.

CARBONARA FRITTATA

5 ounces spaghetti

6 ounces diced guanciale or pancetta, divided

2 tablespoons salted butter

10 large eggs

1¼ cups finely grated Pecorino Romano cheese, plus shaved Pecorino Romano for garnish

¼ cup heavy cream

1 teaspoon freshly cracked black pepper

½ teaspoon sea salt

Arugula, for garnish

1. Preheat the oven to 300°F.

2. Cook the spaghetti according to the package directions until just short of al dente. It will finish cooking in the frittata. Drain and set aside.

3. While the pasta is cooking, heat a 10-inch ovenproof nonstick skillet over medium heat. Cook the guanciale in the skillet until crisp, about 5 minutes. Using a slotted spoon, remove half of the guanciale and set aside for garnish.

4. Add the cooked pasta and the butter to the skillet and cook until the butter is melted and the pasta is completely coated in the butter and rendered fat from the guanciale. Remove the pan from the heat.

5. In a large mixing bowl, whisk the eggs, cheese, cream, pepper, and salt until well incorporated.

6. Pour the egg mixture over the pasta and guanciale in the skillet, making sure that the pasta and guanciale are as evenly distributed as possible. Bake for 30 to 35 minutes, until the frittata is just set in the center and has some spring to the touch.

7. Garnish with the reserved guanciale, shaved Pecorino Romano, and arugula.

TIPS & NOTES

- *The recipe demonstrates my love for creating fun and unique food fusions. I took one of my all-time favorite pasta dishes and turned it into a breakfast dish. This is a great way to use up any kind of leftover pasta.*

- *Pecorino Romano gives the classic carbonara bite, but you can use Parmesan for a milder flavor or Grana Padano for a nuttier touch.*

- *If guanciale or pancetta is unavailable, thick-cut bacon is a great substitute.*

CREAMY TACO PASTA

SERVES: **4**

PREP TIME: **10 MINUTES**

COOK TIME: **40 MINUTES**

1 pound ground beef

2 tablespoons salted butter

3 cloves garlic, minced

¼ cup Taco Seasoning (page 315)

3 tablespoons tomato paste

2 tablespoons Worcestershire sauce

2 cups beef stock

1 cup heavy cream, room temperature

1 (10-ounce) can diced tomatoes and green chilies, with juices

8 ounces medium pasta shells

1 cup shredded sharp white cheddar cheese

1 cup shredded pepper jack cheese

5 ounces Velveeta cheese, cut into cubes

Chopped fresh cilantro, for garnish

1. Preheat a large high-sided skillet or Dutch oven over medium-high heat. Add the ground beef and cook, using a wooden spatula to break up the meat, until browned. Drain the excess grease.

2. Add the butter, garlic, and taco seasoning to the skillet and sauté for 2 to 3 minutes. Add the tomato paste and Worcestershire sauce, stirring to coat the beef mixture evenly. Pour in the stock, cream, and diced tomatoes and green chilies with their juices. Mix well, then add the pasta. Stir to combine and submerge the pasta in the liquid.

3. Bring the mixture to a boil, then reduce the heat to a simmer. Cover and cook, stirring occasionally, until the pasta is tender and has absorbed most of the liquid, 10 to 15 minutes (start checking at the 10-minute mark). Add the cheeses and stir until they are melted and the sauce is smooth and creamy.

4. Let the pasta rest for a couple of minutes to allow the sauce to thicken slightly. Garnish with cilantro before serving.

TIPS & NOTES

- *This is an easy recipe to adapt based on the ingredients you already have on hand. You can use any type of pasta you prefer. Just be sure to adjust the cooking time according to how long that type of pasta needs to cook.*

- *In place of ground beef, try ground pork, chicken, turkey, lamb, or any combination.*

- *You can also swap out the cheddar and pepper jack for any of your favorite cheeses.*

ITALIAN GRINDER PASTA SALAD

SERVES: **6**

PREP TIME: **20 MINUTES, PLUS 30 MINUTES TO CHILL**

COOK TIME: **15 MINUTES**

14 ounces tri-color orecchiette pasta

1 small head romaine lettuce, shredded (about 3 cups)

½ cup chopped marinated artichoke hearts

½ cup cherry tomatoes, quartered

½ cup chopped sliced hard salami

½ cup chopped sliced pepperoni

½ cup chopped sliced ham

⅓ cup finely chopped red onion

⅓ cup thinly sliced pepperoncini

⅓ cup sliced black olives

⅓ cup shredded provolone cheese

⅓ cup crumbled feta cheese

⅓ cup canned chickpeas

FOR THE DRESSING

1 cup mayonnaise

2 tablespoons red wine vinegar

1 tablespoon brine from the pepperoncini jar

2 teaspoons Dijon mustard

2 tablespoons finely grated Parmesan cheese

¾ teaspoon Italian seasoning

1 large clove garlic, grated on a Microplane

½ teaspoon black pepper

¼ teaspoon sea salt

1. Cook the pasta according to the package directions until al dente, then drain.

2. Arrange the pasta and all of the remaining ingredients in a large serving bowl.

3. Put the dressing ingredients in a bowl and whisk to combine.

4. Dress the salad to taste, then toss. Refrigerate for 30 minutes before serving.

> **TIPS & NOTES**
>
> - *This recipe is a take on a grinder sandwich, but in a hearty pasta salad form. It's the perfect dish to bring to a summer cookout.*
>
> - *This recipe is so easy to adapt to whatever ingredients you have on hand. You can use any type of pasta or lettuce you prefer.*
>
> - *Some additional favorite ingredients to mix and match here include Kalamata olives, prosciutto, goat cheese, sharp white cheddar, fresh mozzarella, cucumbers, roasted red peppers, bell peppers, capers, sliced green onions, and fresh basil.*

STREET CORN PASTA SALAD

SERVES: **8**

PREP TIME: **20 MINUTES**

COOK TIME: **20 MINUTES**

4 ears yellow corn, shucked

4 tablespoons salted butter

1½ teaspoons chili powder

1½ teaspoons smoked paprika

¾ teaspoon ground cumin

¾ teaspoon sea salt

½ teaspoon black pepper

10 ounces fusilli pasta

1 cup crumbled goat cheese, divided

⅓ cup finely chopped red onion

1 small red bell pepper, finely chopped (about ⅔ cup)

1 small avocado, peeled, pitted, and diced

FOR GARNISH/SERVING

Cilantro-Lime Avocado Dressing (page 300)

Roughly chopped fresh cilantro

Thinly sliced jalapeño

Paprika

Lime wedges

1. Preheat the oven to 425°F.

2. Lay out four large pieces of aluminum foil. Place an ear of corn in the center of each piece and spread 1 tablespoon of butter over each, covering all of the kernels. In a small bowl, mix the chili powder, paprika, cumin, salt, and pepper. Sprinkle the seasoning mixture generously over the ears of corn.

3. Wrap each ear of corn in the foil, making sure that the sides are completely sealed to prevent the butter from leaking out. You may need to double-wrap each piece. Arrange the wrapped corn on a sheet pan and roast for 20 minutes.

4. While the corn is roasting, cook the pasta according to the package directions, then drain.

5. Let the corn cool for a few minutes. Carefully unwrap each ear, pouring the juices into a large mixing bowl. Cut the corn kernels off the cobs (you should have about 3 cups) and add them to the bowl with the juices.

6. Add the cooked pasta and ¾ cup of the goat cheese to the corn. Mix until the cheese has melted into the corn juices. Stir in the onion, bell pepper, and avocado. Pour in the desired amount of dressing and toss to combine.

7. Top the salad with a drizzle of dressing and the remaining ¼ cup of goat cheese. Garnish with cilantro, jalapeño, and/or a sprinkle of paprika and serve with lime wedges.

TIPS & NOTES

- *If you want extra smoky flavor, grill the corn instead of roasting it. You can also char the kernels in a dry cast-iron skillet after cutting them off the cob.*

- *For added texture, toss in some crushed tortilla chips or roasted pepitas before serving.*

- *Goat cheese adds a tangy creaminess, but you can swap it for feta, Cotija, or queso fresco for a more traditional elote-style salad. For a milder option, use shredded Monterey Jack.*

HOMEMADE
BASICS

There's a special kind of magic in making the building blocks of flavor from scratch. I promise that once you start doing it, you will never want to go back to store-bought versions.

It's the simple act of combining everyday ingredients to turn them into something special, like a zesty aioli that brings steamed artichokes to life, a creamy salad dressing that perfectly coats every leaf of a salad, or a seasoning blend that turns boring chicken into the star of the show.

Here, you'll find a collection of sauces, dips, dressings, confits, and seasoning blends, all tried, true, and endlessly adaptable. If you're the kind of cook who likes to use a recipe as a guideline to make something your own, consider this chapter your playground.

WHY MAKE YOUR OWN BASICS?

Cost-effective: Making your own kitchen staples is often more economical in the long run, especially when you have a well-stocked pantry. You'll be surprised at how much you save compared to buying commercial products.

Adaptability: When you make your own, you can tailor the flavors to your exact preferences. Whether you like it spicier, sweeter, or tangier, you have full control over salt, sugar, spices, acid, and oils, ensuring you create your perfect flavor profile every time.

Cleaner ingredients: Homemade versions let you skip the additives, preservatives, fillers, and artificial ingredients commonly found in store-bought products. You'll be using fresh, whole ingredients, which not only taste better but are better for you.

Allergy-friendly: When you make your own basics, you have the freedom to omit or substitute ingredients that may trigger food allergies or sensitivities, like dairy, gluten, or eggs.

Customizable portions: Homemade basics allow you to scale recipes based on how many servings you want, ensuring you never end up with too much or too little, as well as helping to reduce food waste.

Less packaging waste: Homemade basics reduce the need for store-bought versions that come in single-use plastic. Making your own condiments and opting for reusable containers at home is much more eco-friendly.

Each recipe in this chapter focuses on enhancing flavor. Whether it is nutty caramelized roasted garlic to spread on toasted sourdough, a seasoning blend that takes your eggs to a whole new level, or a briny olive salad to pile high on top of chicken, every recipe is meant to complement and enhance all of the recipes throughout the book. You'll also find tips for substitutions, storage, and ways to use these versatile basics beyond their obvious roles.

Now let's dive into the flavor, shall we?

CILANTRO-LIME AVOCADO DRESSING

1 small avocado, pitted and peeled

2 cloves garlic, peeled

½ cup mayonnaise

½ cup Mexican crema or sour cream

¼ cup crumbled goat cheese

¼ cup loosely packed fresh cilantro leaves

¼ teaspoon sea salt, or more to taste

½ teaspoon black pepper

Put all of the ingredients in a food processor or high-powered blender and pulse until smooth. Store in the refrigerator for up to 2 weeks.

TIPS & NOTES

- *This makes an excellent salad dressing or a sauce for tacos, seafood dishes, and even chicken salad. It's very versatile.*

- *If you are not a fan of cilantro, this dressing is also delicious made with basil or parsley.*

- *In place of the goat cheese, you can use feta or Cotija.*

- *Use in Chicken Tacos (page 72) and Street Corn Pasta Salad (page 294).*

LEMON-CAPER AIOLI

MAKES: **ABOUT 1½ CUPS**

PREP TIME: **5 MINUTES**

1 cup mayonnaise

¼ cup capers, drained

4 cloves garlic, minced

2 teaspoons Dijon mustard

2 teaspoons fresh lemon juice

½ teaspoon onion powder

Sea salt and black pepper, to taste

Put all of the ingredients in a medium mixing bowl and mix until well incorporated. Refrigerate for 1 to 2 hours before serving. Store in the refrigerator for up to 2 weeks.

TIPS & NOTES

- *Add a little bit of fresh horseradish to make a spicy version.*

- *Try chives in place of (or in addition to) the capers.*

- *Other flavor combos: tomato and basil, pesto, cilantro and lime, chipotle and lime.*

- *Serve with Steamed Artichokes (page 162), Pasta Chips (page 264), or even the Tuna Melt Fritters (page 252).*

CAPER-DILL HOLLANDAISE

MAKES: **1 BATCH**

PREP TIME: **10 MINUTES**

COOK TIME: **10 MINUTES**

4 large egg yolks

2 tablespoons fresh lemon juice

½ cup (1 stick) salted butter, melted

2 tablespoons capers, drained

1 tablespoon chopped fresh dill, plus extra for garnish

Pinch of cayenne pepper

Pinch of sea salt

Dash of hot sauce

1. In a stainless-steel mixing bowl, whisk the egg yolks and lemon juice until thick and increased in volume.

2. Set up a double-boiler: Place a saucepan with 1 to 2 inches of water over medium heat until the water is simmering. Reduce the heat to medium-low. Place the bowl over the top of the saucepan, making sure that the water is not touching the bottom of the bowl (or the eggs will begin to scramble).

3. Whisking rapidly, add the melted butter little by little, until the sauce has thickened and is light and fluffy.

4. Remove the bowl from the pan and gently fold in the capers, dill, cayenne, salt, and hot sauce. This is best served immediately.

TIPS & NOTES

- *Hollandaise is one of my favorite sauces to enjoy not only on breakfast dishes, but also with seafood and vegetables.*

- *For a traditional hollandaise, simply omit the capers and dill.*

- *Use in Crab and Shrimp–Stuffed Salmon (page 71).*

AVOCADO RANCH DRESSING

MAKES: **ABOUT 1¾ CUPS**

PREP TIME: **10 MINUTES**

1 small avocado, peeled and pitted

½ cup mayonnaise

½ cup sour cream

2 teaspoons apple cider vinegar

1 tablespoon chopped fresh flat-leaf parsley

1 tablespoon chopped fresh chives

1 teaspoon chopped fresh dill

1 clove garlic, minced

½ teaspoon onion powder

¼ teaspoon sea salt

Put all of the ingredients in a food processor or high-powered blender and pulse until smooth. Store in the refrigerator for up to 2 weeks.

TIPS & NOTES

To vary the flavor, omit the avocado and add some crispy chopped bacon to make a bacon ranch dressing; or add buffalo sauce to taste for a buffalo ranch dressing. It's also delicious with the addition of blue cheese crumbles for a hybrid of ranch and blue cheese dressing.

RUSSIAN DRESSING

MAKES: **ABOUT 1¾ CUPS**

PREP TIME: **5 MINUTES**

1 cup mayonnaise

½ cup ketchup

2 tablespoons spicy brown mustard

1 tablespoon Worcestershire sauce

1 tablespoon chopped fresh parsley

1 tablespoon chopped fresh chives

1 teaspoon chopped fresh dill

Put all of the ingredients in a small mixing bowl and mix until well incorporated. Store in the refrigerator for up to 2 weeks.

TIPS & NOTES

Use in Reuben Egg Rolls (page 104).

CAESAR DRESSING

MAKES: **ABOUT 1¾ CUPS**

PREP TIME: **10 MINUTES**

1 cup mayonnaise

⅓ cup finely grated Parmesan cheese

2 tablespoons fresh lemon juice

4 cloves garlic, minced

3 anchovy fillets, minced

1 tablespoon Worcestershire sauce

1 teaspoon Dijon mustard

½ teaspoon sea salt

½ teaspoon ground black pepper

Put all of the ingredients in a small mixing bowl and whisk to combine. Store in the refrigerator for up to 2 weeks.

> **TIPS & NOTES**
>
> *Use in Kale, Spinach, and Romaine Caesar (page 207) and Caesar Salad Breakfast Toast (page 233).*

BURGER SAUCE

MAKES: **1 CUP**

PREP TIME: **5 MINUTES**

½ cup mayonnaise

2 tablespoons ketchup

1 small dill pickle, finely chopped

2 tablespoons dill pickle juice

2 teaspoons hot sauce

1 teaspoon Dijon mustard

1 teaspoon Worcestershire sauce

1 teaspoon dried minced onion

1 clove garlic, minced, or ½ teaspoon garlic powder

¼ teaspoon black pepper

Put all of the ingredients in a mixing bowl and whisk until well combined. Store in the refrigerator for up to 2 weeks.

> **TIPS & NOTES**
>
> - *Whether you call it fry sauce, burger sauce, secret sauce, mac sauce, or any other name, this will definitely become your go-to condiment. If you omit the hot sauce and include the chopped pickles, it also makes a fantastic Thousand Island dressing.*
>
> - *Use in Sloppy Macs (page 100) and Burger Board (page 204).*

YUM YUM SAUCE

1 cup mayonnaise

2 tablespoons ketchup

1 tablespoon plus 1 teaspoon powdered sugar or other sweetener of choice

1 tablespoon unseasoned rice vinegar

1 tablespoon salted butter, melted

2 teaspoons sriracha (optional)

1½ teaspoons garlic powder

½ teaspoon onion powder

½ teaspoon paprika

Water, if needed

Put all of the ingredients except the water in a mixing bowl and whisk until well incorporated. Add water a teaspoon at a time until the sauce has reached your desired consistency. Store in the refrigerator for up to 2 weeks.

TIPS & NOTES

If you've made my famous Egg Roll in a Bowl recipe from my site, or from my book Craveable Keto, *then you have likely made my Yum Yum Sauce. It is such a versatile condiment: It is delicious on Asian-inspired recipes, as a salad dressing, as a dip, on seafood, you name it. In this book, it pairs excellently with Furikake Potato Wedges (page 260), Egg Roll Burgers (page 107), Tuna Melt Fritters (page 252), and California Roll in a Bowl (page 211).*

CUCUMBER SAUCE

MAKES: **ABOUT 1½ CUPS**

PREP TIME: **10 MINUTES**

1 mini seedless cucumber, sliced

½ cup sour cream

¼ cup mayonnaise

2 tablespoons fresh lemon juice

2 tablespoons chopped fresh chives

1 tablespoon chopped fresh dill

1 teaspoon chopped fresh mint

2 cloves garlic, minced

½ teaspoon sea salt

¼ teaspoon black pepper

Put all of the ingredients in a blender or food processor and pulse until smooth and creamy. Store in the refrigerator for up to 2 weeks.

TIPS & NOTES

Use in Loaded Greek Fries (page 263).

OLIVE SALAD

1½ cups giardiniera pickled vegetables

1 cup green olives with pimentos

1 cup Kalamata olives

½ cup pepperoncini

⅓ cup red wine vinegar

¼ cup olive oil

¼ cup roasted red peppers

4 large cloves garlic

1 teaspoon dried oregano

1 teaspoon dried basil

½ teaspoon black pepper

½ cup capers, drained

Put all of the ingredients except the capers in a food processor and pulse until everything is roughly chopped and well incorporated. Stir in the capers. Cover and refrigerate for at least 1 hour before serving. Store in the refrigerator for up to 2 weeks.

TIPS & NOTES

Use in Muffuletta Chicken (page 63).

ROASTED GARLIC TWO WAYS

GARLIC CONFIT

MAKES: **1 BATCH**

PREP TIME: **15 MINUTES**

COOK TIME: **2 HOURS**

1 cup peeled garlic cloves

Fresh herbs (such as rosemary or thyme) (optional)

Dried chile pods (optional)

1½ cups olive oil

1. Preheat the oven to 250°F.

2. Combine the garlic cloves with the herbs and chile pods, if using, in a mini Dutch oven or other ovenproof dish. Pour the olive oil over the top, completely submerging the garlic. Cover and bake for 2 to 2½ hours, until the garlic cloves are soft and a light caramel color.

3. Discard the herbs and strain the oil through a fine-mesh sieve. Transfer the garlic to a jar and add the strained oil, completely submerging the garlic cloves. Secure the lid and store in the fridge for up to 3 weeks, making certain that the garlic cloves stay below the level of the oil for safe storage.

WHOLE ROASTED GARLIC

MAKES: **1 BATCH**

PREP TIME: **5 MINUTES**

COOK TIME: **45 MINUTES**

4 large heads garlic, unpeeled

¼ cup olive oil, divided

1 teaspoon sea salt

4 sprigs fresh thyme

TIPS & NOTES

Use either Garlic Confit or Whole Roasted Garlic in Mississippi Pot Roast Grilled Cheese (page 330) or on toast (see the Toasts chapter beginning on page 218). Use Whole Roasted Garlic to make Roasted Garlic Mashed Potatoes (page 189).

1. Preheat the oven to 400°F.

2. Cut the top ¼ to ½ inch off of each head of garlic, exposing the cloves but leaving them in place within their peels. Place each head on a sheet of aluminum foil that is large enough to wrap around the entire head of garlic. Drizzle each head with 1 tablespoon of olive oil, sprinkle with ¼ teaspoon of salt, and top with a sprig of thyme. Wrap each bulb tightly in the foil.

3. Put the foil packets on a sheet pan and bake for 45 minutes, or until the garlic cloves are tender and caramelized to a rich brown color.

TOMATO CONFIT

MAKES: **1 BATCH**

PREP TIME: **10 MINUTES**

COOK TIME: **2 HOURS**

1½ pounds cherry or grape tomatoes

1 head garlic, top ¼ inch cut off

1½ cups olive oil

½ teaspoon red pepper flakes

Sea salt and black pepper

1. Preheat the oven to 250°F.

2. Arrange the tomatoes and garlic in a single layer in a baking dish. Drizzle the olive oil over the tomatoes and garlic, sprinkle with the red pepper flakes, and season generously with salt and pepper.

3. Bake uncovered for 2 hours, or until the tomatoes are soft and wrinkly but not bursting. The tomatoes will keep in the refrigerator for up to 2 weeks. Add leftover tomatoes to a jar and pour over the leftover oil. If there is not enough oil leftover to submerge the tomatoes, add fresh olive oil to cover.

WAYS TO USE TOMATO CONFIT

- *Make Tomato Confit Toast (page 242).*

- *Serve it on a charcuterie board.*

- *Use it as a topping for sandwiches, burgers, and paninis, or for grilled chicken, fish, or pork.*

- *Incorporate it into omelets or frittatas for a savory breakfast.*

- *Use it as a pizza topping.*

- *Add some of the roasted tomatoes to homemade hummus for a rich, mellow tomatoey flavor.*

- *Mix leftover tomato infused oil with some vinegar, Dijon mustard, garlic, oregano, salt, and pepper to make a vinaigrette.*

HERBY EVERYTHING SEASONING

MAKES: **ABOUT 1¼ CUPS**

PREP TIME: **5 MINUTES**

¼ cup white and black sesame seeds

3 tablespoons plus 1 teaspoon dried minced onion

3 tablespoons plus 1 teaspoon dried minced garlic

3 tablespoons poppy seeds

2 tablespoons coarse sea salt

2 tablespoons freeze-dried chives

2 tablespoons freeze-dried parsley

1 tablespoon plus 2 teaspoons freeze-dried dill

Put all of the ingredients in an airtight jar. Shake well before using.

TIPS & NOTES

- *This is my all-time favorite seasoning blend. My preferred way to enjoy it is on eggs, as you will see throughout the Toast chapter.*

- *Use in Freezer Breakfast Sandwiches (page 127).*

BLACKENED SEASONING

MAKES: **ABOUT ⅓ CUP**

PREP TIME: **5 MINUTES**

1½ tablespoons smoked paprika

1 tablespoon garlic powder

1 tablespoon onion powder

1 tablespoon dried thyme leaves

1 teaspoon cayenne pepper

1 teaspoon dried basil

1 teaspoon celery salt

1 teaspoon ground cumin

½ teaspoon dried oregano

Put all of the ingredients in an airtight jar. Shake well before using.

TIPS & NOTES

Use in Roasted Blackened Chicken and Vegetables (page 66) and Blackened Mahi Mahi with Pineapple Salsa (page 115).

TACO SEASONING

MAKES: **ABOUT 10 TABLESPOONS**

PREP TIME: **5 MINUTES**

3 tablespoons chili powder

3 tablespoons ground cumin

1 tablespoon celery salt

1 tablespoon garlic powder

1 tablespoon onion powder

¾ teaspoon black pepper

¾ teaspoon cayenne pepper

¾ teaspoon sea salt

Put all of the ingredients in an airtight jar. Shake well before using.

TIPS & NOTES

- *This taco seasoning is a tad on the spicy side. If you do not care for spicy foods, simply reduce or omit the cayenne pepper.*

- *Use ¼ cup seasoning for each pound of meat.*

- *Use in Chicken Tacos (page 72) and Creamy Taco Pasta (page 290).*

REPURPOSING
LEFTOVERS

I could write an entire cookbook about repurposing leftovers. Or, at the very least, supplemental guides to all of my cookbooks detailing ideas for turning the leftovers from yesterday's dinner into today's breakfast, lunch, or dinner.

Leftovers can be a hidden gem in your kitchen, offering an opportunity to save money, reduce waste, and make quick, delicious meals without starting from scratch. It is all about maximizing the life of your food by transforming leftovers into meals that are fresh, flavorful, and new.

This doesn't just mean reheating last night's dinner. Instead, it's about turning those extra portions into completely new dishes—whether it is something as simple as turning leftover flank steak into Flank Steak Tacos (page 325), or using Mississippi Pot Roast (page 174) to make a Mississippi Pot Roast Grilled Cheese (page 330), or something a little more complex, like using leftover pulled pork to make Pulled Pork–Stuffed Sweet Potatoes (page 322). These all showcase that leftovers don't have to be boring and repetitive. With a bit of creativity, a well-stocked pantry, and some planning, the possibilities are endless.

I first offer half a dozen full-fledged recipes that utilize leftovers from one of the other recipes in the book. Then, in the pages that follow, I list quick ideas for repurposing leftovers for two dozen other recipes. Once you get the hang of it, your leftover meals will only get more and more creative. I can't wait to see what you come up with on your own. So, let's get started transforming your leftovers into meals that feel fresh, exciting, and completely different from the original dish.

QUESABIRRIA TACOS

SERVES: **4**

PREP TIME: **10 MINUTES**

COOK TIME: **20 MINUTES**

If you've never tried quesabirria tacos, you're in for a treat. Think crispy, cheesy tacos packed with tender, slow-cooked birria beef and served with the rich, flavorful birria consommé for dipping. They're messy in all the best ways—crispy edges, gooey cheese, and that juicy, savory beef.

3 cups leftover shredded Beef Birria (page 138), plus ¼ cup of the oil skimmed from the top of the cooked birria

8 corn tortillas

2 cups shredded Monterey Jack cheese

Leftover birria consommé, for dipping

1. Heat 2 teaspoons of the birria oil in a large skillet over medium heat. Lay a tortilla in the pan and swirl it around to coat it in the oil. Flip it over and do the same thing on the other side.

2. With the tortilla still in the pan, add about 2 tablespoons of cheese to one half of the tortilla and let it melt. Top with some of the shredded beef and then another 2 tablespoons of cheese. Fold the tortilla in half. Flip the taco over and cook for 2 to 3 minutes, until crispy on the bottom. Flip it over once more and cook for 1 to 2 minutes, until crispy on the other side. Set the taco aside on a cooling rack.

3. Repeat the process with the remaining ingredients. Serve the tacos with leftover birria consommé, for dipping.

> **TIPS & NOTES**
>
> • *See page 334 for more birria leftover ideas.*

PULLED PORK–STUFFED SWEET POTATOES

SERVES: **4**

PREP TIME: **10 MINUTES**

COOK TIME: **55 MINUTES**

Sweet potatoes meet savory pulled pork in this hearty dish that's both satisfying and full of flavor. Topped with melted pepper jack cheese, Mexican crema, salsa verde, creamy avocado, and Cotija cheese, each bite is a perfect balance of sweet, smoky, and tangy. Garnished with pickled red onions, jalapeños, and fresh cilantro, these stuffed potatoes are a delicious way to repurpose leftover pulled pork into a comforting meal.

4 medium sweet potatoes

Sea salt and black pepper

1 cup shredded pepper jack cheese

2½ cups leftover Pulled Pork (page 181)

⅓ cup Mexican crema or sour cream

½ cup salsa verde

1 large avocado, pitted, peeled, and thinly sliced

⅓ cup Cotija cheese

1 large Roma tomato, diced

FOR GARNISH/SERVING

1 small jalapeño, thinly sliced

Pickled red onions

Torn fresh cilantro

Lime wedges

1. Preheat the oven to 425°F. Line a sheet pan with parchment paper.

2. Use a fork to poke holes in the sweet potatoes. Place on the prepared pan and bake for 45 minutes, or until soft inside when pierced with a fork. Cut the sweet potatoes in half lengthwise. Use a fork to rake over the top, loosening the flesh. Create a well in the center for the toppings. Sprinkle each one with a little salt and pepper.

3. Top each sweet potato half with some of the pepper jack cheese and pulled pork. Return to the oven and bake for 5 minutes, or until the cheese is melted and the pork is warmed through.

4. Top the sweet potato halves with the Mexican crema, salsa verde, avocado, Cotija cheese, and tomatoes. Garnish with the jalapeño, pickled onions, and cilantro and serve with lime slices on the side.

FLANK STEAK TACOS

These flavorful tacos are a perfect way to repurpose leftover Chili-Lime Flank Steak and Grilled Corn Salsa. With charred flour tortillas filled with tender steak, zesty corn salsa, and creamy toppings, they're a quick and satisfying meal. Add a variety of customizable toppings like guacamole, sour cream, and Cotija cheese for a taco bar experience everyone will love. It's a fun and easy way to breathe new life into yesterday's dinner.

8 small flour tortillas

2 servings leftover Chili-Lime Flank Steak (page 98)

1½ cups leftover Grilled Corn Salsa (page 98)

½ cup guacamole

½ cup sour cream

½ cup Cotija cheese

Pickled red onions

Chopped fresh cilantro

1 lime, cut into wedges, for serving

1. Preheat a skillet or grill pan over medium heat. One at a time, lightly char the tortillas for about 30 seconds per side, until warm and slightly crisped. Keep them wrapped in a clean kitchen towel to stay warm.

2. Slice the steak into thin strips. Gently reheat in a skillet over medium heat until warmed through, 2 to 3 minutes.

3. Place a few strips of the reheated steak in the center of each tortilla. Top with the corn salsa, guacamole, sour cream, Cotija, pickled onions, and cilantro. Serve with lime wedges.

CHILI CHEESE EGG MUFFINS

SERVES: **4**

PREP TIME: **10 MINUTES**

COOK TIME: **25 MINUTES**

Repurpose leftover Kickin' Chili in these hearty, cheesy egg muffins. Perfect for breakfast, brunch, or even a quick lunch, these muffins are packed with savory chili and cheddar cheese, making them a satisfying way to use up extra chili. Topped with sour cream, extra cheddar, and green onions, they offer a cozy, flavorful start to the day or a delicious snack anytime.

12 large eggs

2 cups leftover Kickin' Chili (page 178), divided

1 cup shredded sharp cheddar cheese, plus extra for garnish

1 small yellow onion, diced

1 teaspoon sea salt

½ teaspoon black pepper

¼ cup sour cream

Thinly sliced green onions, for garnish

1. Preheat the oven to 350°F. Lightly grease the 12 cups of a standard-sized muffin tin.

2. Divide 1½ cups of the chili evenly among the wells of the muffin tin.

3. Crack the eggs into a large mixing bowl and whisk with a fork. Mix in the cheddar, onion, salt, and pepper. Divide the egg mixture evenly among the prepared muffin cups. Stir slightly to mix the chili into the eggs.

4. Bake for 20 to 25 minutes, until the egg muffins are light and fluffy and cooked all the way through. Top the egg muffins with some of the remaining ½ cup of chili and the sour cream. Garnish with additional cheddar and green onions before serving.

CHICKEN POT PIE PIZZA

SERVES: **4**

PREP TIME: **30 MINUTES, PLUS 30 MINUTES TO REST**

COOK TIME: **30 MINUTES**

This indulgent twist on chicken pot pie takes the cozy comfort of a creamy, savory filling and layers it on top of a crispy pizza crust. Perfect for repurposing leftover roasted chicken (see page 339 for more ideas), it transforms simple ingredients into a hearty and satisfying dish. You can customize it with extra veggies or a different cheese blend to suit your taste.

Olive oil

1 (16-ounce) package refrigerated pizza dough

4 tablespoons salted butter, divided

½ cup diced carrots, divided

⅓ cup diced celery

⅓ cup diced onion

2 cloves garlic, minced

½ teaspoon dried thyme, divided

½ teaspoon sea salt

½ teaspoon black pepper

10 ounces leftover Lemon-Herb Roasted Chicken (page 145)

1 cup heavy cream

¼ cup chicken stock

1 tablespoon Dijon mustard

¾ cup shredded sharp cheddar cheese

½ cup shredded Italian cheese blend

⅓ cup frozen green peas

5 tablespoons grated Parmesan cheese, divided

1. Drizzle a bit of olive oil on the bottom of a mixing bowl. Form the pizza dough into a ball and place in the bowl. Drizzle a little oil on top of the dough. Cover the bowl and let the dough rest at room temperature for at least 30 minutes.

2. While the dough is resting, make the pot pie topping: Melt 2 tablespoons of the butter with 1 tablespoon of olive oil in a large skillet over medium heat. Add ⅓ cup of the carrots, the celery, onion, garlic, ¼ teaspoon of the thyme, the salt, and pepper and sauté until the vegetables are tender, about 8 minutes. Add the chicken and cook until it is warmed through. Pour in the cream, stock, and mustard and bring to a boil over medium-high heat. Reduce the heat to low and let simmer for 5 to 7 minutes, stirring occasionally. Mix in the cheddar until melted and simmer until the sauce has reduced and thickened, about 5 minutes.

3. Preheat the oven to 400°F.

4. Place the dough on a pizza pan and stretch it into an even 14-inch round, making a lip around the edge. Ladle three-quarters of the pot pie topping onto the dough and spread into an even layer. Top with the Italian cheese. Dollop the remaining topping over the cheese. Sprinkle the peas, reserved carrots, and Parmesan cheese on top.

5. Bake for 15 minutes, or until the crust is golden brown and the cheese is melted and bubbly.

6. Melt the remaining 2 tablespoons of butter. Mix together the melted butter, remaining tablespoon of Parmesan, and remaining ¼ teaspoon of thyme in a small bowl and brush over the crust before serving.

MISSISSIPPI POT ROAST GRILLED CHEESE

A comforting, indulgent twist on the classic grilled cheese, this version is loaded with savory leftover Mississippi Pot Roast, melty cheeses, and a touch of tangy pepperoncini. The garlic-infused butter spread adds extra depth to the crispy, golden bread, making each bite irresistibly delicious. If you have extra juice from the pot roast, it is delicious as a dip for the sandwich—like an extra flavorful au jus.

3 tablespoons salted butter, softened

2 cloves Garlic Confit (page 310) or Whole Roasted Garlic (page 311)

2 tablespoons freshly grated Parmesan cheese

4 large slices sourdough bread

1 cup shredded leftover Mississippi Pot Roast (page 174)

3 pepperoncini, thinly sliced

½ cup shredded Gruyère cheese

½ cup shredded mozzarella cheese

1. In a small bowl, combine the butter, garlic confit, and Parmesan. Spread this mixture generously on one side of each slice of bread.

2. Preheat a large skillet over medium heat. Place one slice of bread, buttered side down, in the pan. Layer with half of the shredded pot roast, followed by half of the pepperoncini. Top with half of the Gruyère and mozzarella. Top with the second slice of bread, buttered side up. Cook for 3 to 4 minutes on the first side, pressing gently with a spatula, until the bread is golden brown. Flip and cook for an additional 3 to 4 minutes, until the other side is golden brown and the cheese is fully melted. Remove from the skillet and let rest for a minute before slicing in half to serve.

3. Repeat the steps to make the second sandwich.

MORE IDEAS FOR
REPURPOSING LEFTOVERS

With a little creativity, leftovers can be transformed into fresh, exciting dishes. The key to repurposing leftovers is to look at them with a new perspective: they're not just remnants of a meal, they're the building blocks of something delicious. In this section, you'll find clever ways to reinvent your leftovers with bold flavors, unexpected pairings, and novel presentations. No need to settle for reheating the same meal when you can turn it into something entirely new!

Each suggestion here is designed with versatility in mind. It's about taking what you already have and making it work in a fresh way—whether it's turning roasted veggies into a savory breakfast hash or using extra steak in a vibrant grain bowl. The idea is simple: keep the core ingredients from your original meal, but play with their presentation, flavor, and texture to create something that feels brand-new.

BAKED HAM and EGG SKILLET

· **Ham and Egg Croissant Sandwich:** *Layer leftover ham, eggs, and cheese between a toasted split croissant and add a spoonful of pesto.*

· **Ham and Egg Salad:** *Chop leftover ham and eggs and mix with chopped lettuce, green olives, fresh herbs, and a light vinaigrette.*

BAKED HEIRLOOM CAPRESE with WARM BACON VINAIGRETTE

· **Caprese BLT Flatbread:** *Use leftover roasted tomatoes, mozzarella, and bacon for a flavorful flatbread. Spread a thin layer of Garlic Confit (page 310) and pesto on naan or flatbread. Top with the leftover caprese ingredients, bake at 375°F for 8 to 10 minutes until the cheese is melted, and finish with fresh basil and a drizzle of balsamic glaze.*

· **Caprese Stuffed Chicken:** *Stuff chicken breasts with the leftover roasted tomatoes, fresh mozzarella, and a little bacon. Secure the breasts with toothpicks and bake at 375°F for 25 to 30 minutes, or until the chicken is cooked through. Drizzle the remaining bacon vinaigrette over the top before serving.*

· **Heirloom Caprese Quiche:** *Whisk together 4 eggs and ½ cup cream (or your preferred milk), season with salt and pepper. Pour the egg mixture into a prepared pie crust, then stir in the leftover roasted tomatoes, fresh mozzarella, crumbled bacon, and fresh basil leaves. Bake at 350°F for 35 to 40 minutes, or until set in the center.*

BALSAMIC PESTO BEEF KABOBS

· **Balsamic Pesto Beef Wraps:** *Use the leftover beef and veggies as a filling for a wrap. Add some leafy greens like spinach or arugula, and drizzle with a bit more balsamic pesto vinaigrette. Add slices of fresh mozzarella and avocado.*

· **Beef Kabob Grain Bowl:** *Create a grain bowl with the leftover beef and vegetables. Add a base of quinoa, farro, or rice, and top with the leftover kabob ingredients. Drizzle with any remaining balsamic pesto vinaigrette. You can add roasted chickpeas, sun-dried tomatoes, and some pickled onions to elevate the dish.*

· **Beef and Vegetable Fried Rice:** *Chop up the leftover beef and vegetables and stir-fry with cooked rice. Add some soy sauce, scrambled eggs, and a bit of sesame oil for a quick fried rice dish. Garnish with chopped green onions and a sprinkle of sesame seeds for extra flavor.*

BALSAMIC SHORT RIBS

· **Short Rib Pot Pie:** *Shred leftover short ribs and use as the filling for a savory pot pie, mixing the meat with vegetables and leftover shallot gravy. Top with a frozen pie crust dough and bake as per the directions.*

· **Short Rib Poutine:** *Top crispy fries with shredded leftover short ribs and cheese curds, then pour leftover shallot gravy over the top.*

BEEF BIRRIA

· **Birria Mac and Cheese:** *Make a creamy mac and cheese and stir in shredded leftover birria beef for a rich, flavorful twist. Drizzle some of the consommé over the top for added flavor.*

· **Birria Nachos:** *Layer tortilla chips with shredded leftover birria beef, melted mozzarella or Monterey Jack cheese, and a drizzle of the leftover birria consommé. Top with chopped onions, fresh cilantro, and a squeeze of lime.*

· *See also* **Quesabirria Tacos**, *page 321.*

BLACKENED MAHI MAHI with PINEAPPLE SALSA

· **Blackened Mahi Pineapple Quesadillas:** *Combine the leftover mahi mahi with cheese (like Monterey Jack or mozzarella) and a spoonful of the pineapple salsa. Spread the mixture between two tortillas and grill until crispy and golden brown on both sides. Serve with sour cream or guacamole for dipping.*

· **Fish Tacos:** *Flake the leftover mahi mahi and use it as the filling for soft tacos. Add a spoonful of the pineapple salsa, some shredded cabbage or lettuce, and a drizzle of crema or sour cream. Squeeze a little extra lime juice on top to bring out the brightness of the salsa.*

· **Mahi Mahi Power Bowls:** *Serve flaked leftover mahi mahi over a bowl of cilantro lime rice. Add leftover pineapple salsa, avocado slices, black beans, and a sprinkle of toasted pepitas.*

CABBAGE ROLL IN A BOWL

· **Cabbage Roll Casserole:** Layer the leftover cabbage roll filling in a baking dish, top with shredded cheese, and bake at 375°F for 20 to 25 minutes until bubbly and golden. This creates a comforting casserole version of the original dish.

· **Cabbage Roll Soup:** Turn the leftover cabbage roll filling into a comforting soup. Add some extra beef stock or broth to thin it out, bring to a simmer, and serve with a sprinkle of fresh parsley. You could even add extra vegetables like carrots or celery if desired.

· **Cabbage Roll Stuffed Peppers:** Hollow out bell peppers and stuff them with the leftover cabbage roll filling. Place them in a baking dish, cover with foil, and bake at 375°F for 25 to 30 minutes until the peppers are tender. Top with a little cheese (optional) and bake uncovered for an additional 5 minutes until melted.

CHILI-LIME FLANK STEAK with GRILLED CORN SALSA

· **Chili-Lime Steak Sandwiches:** Spread some chimichurri on a crusty sandwich roll. Thinly slice the leftover steak and pile it onto the roll. Top with corn salsa, avocado, and some Cotija cheese for a delicious, hearty sandwich.

· **Steak and Corn–Stuffed Sweet Potatoes:** Roast sweet potatoes until tender, then slice open and stuff with leftover steak and corn salsa. Top with cheese, avocado, and sour cream.

· **Steak Nachos:** Spread tortilla chips on a sheet pan and top with chopped leftover steak, and shredded mozzarella cheese. Then sprinkle over the leftover salsa. Bake at 375°F for 10 to 15 minutes, until the cheese is melted and bubbly. Keep an eye on them after 10 minutes to make sure the chips don't get too crispy. Garnish with sour cream, jalapeños, and cilantro.

CREAMY CHICKEN MARSALA

· **Chicken Marsala Pizza:** Spread leftover marsala sauce over pizza dough, then top with shredded leftover chicken and mushrooms and shredded mozzarella cheese. Bake at 400°F for 15 to 20 minutes, until the crust is golden brown on the edges and cooked in the center. Sprinkle with fresh thyme or parsley.

· **Chicken Marsala Sandwiches:** Layer leftover chicken with leftover marsala sauce on toasted croissants or hoagie rolls. Top with sharp white cheddar cheese and some arugula.

CUBAN POTATO SKINS

- **Cuban Breakfast Skillet:** *Slice the leftover potatoes and toss them into a hot skillet. Add leftover pulled pork, ham, and cheese, then crack a couple of eggs on top. Cook until the eggs are set, then serve with sliced pickles and chives.*

- **Cuban Croquettes:** *Mash leftover potato skins with chopped leftover toppings. Shape into patties, then coat in beaten egg and then in breadcrumbs. Fry until golden and crispy. Serve with mustard dipping sauce or aioli.*

- **Cuban Potato Soup:** *Use the leftover scooped-out potato and combine it with some chicken stock. Use an immersion blender to create a creamy potato soup base. Stir in the pulled pork, melted Swiss cheese, and a touch of Dijon mustard, salt, pepper, garlic powder, and onion powder, to taste for a Cuban-inspired flavor.*

FRENCH ONION CHICKEN

- **French Onion Chicken Pasta:** *Combine chopped leftover chicken and leftover onions and gravy and toss with cooked pasta. Add a splash of heavy cream and beef stock and finish with thyme and grated Parmesan.*

- **French Onion Chicken Quesadillas:** *Chop up chicken and onions and spread across a tortilla, then top with Gruyère and another tortilla. Pan-fry until golden brown and crispy. Serve with a side of sour cream.*

- **French Onion Chicken Rice Bowl:** *Serve reheated chicken and onions over a bed of fluffy white rice, cauliflower rice, or even quinoa. Add a drizzle of leftover sauce and a sprinkle of fresh thyme for a quick and hearty bowl.*

- **French Onion Chicken Stuffed Potatoes:** *Scoop out the insides of baked potatoes and mix with shredded leftover chicken, onions, and a little additional Gruyère and/or mozzarella cheese. Stuff the mixture back into the potato shells, top with more Gruyère, and broil until bubbly.*

GARLIC BUTTER STEAK BITES

· **Garlic Steak Fried Rice:** *Chop leftover steak bites into smaller pieces and toss into fried rice with scrambled eggs, peas, carrots, and green onions. Add soy sauce, garlic, and a dash of sesame oil.*

· **Steak Salad:** *Chop the leftover steak bites and toss them with mixed greens, pickled red onion, cherry tomatoes, avocado, roasted vegetables and crumbled blue cheese. Dress with Balsamic Pesto Vinaigrette (page 96) or Avocado Ranch Dressing (page 304).*

· **Steak Tacos:** *Warm the leftover steak bites and use them as the filling for tacos. Add sautéed onions and bell peppers, and top with sour cream, guacamole, or salsa. Add some chopped fresh cilantro and a squeeze of lime for a burst of freshness.*

GARLIC PARMESAN CHICKEN SKEWERS

· **Garlic Parmesan Chicken Fried Rice:** *Stir-fry diced leftover chicken with rice, peas, carrots, and scrambled eggs. Add a little soy sauce and a touch of the garlic butter sauce for extra flavor.*

· **Garlic Parmesan Chicken Pasta:** *Toss sliced leftover chicken with cooked pasta, sautéed spinach, and additional garlic butter sauce. Top with Parmesan and a squeeze of lemon.*

GNOCCHI with PANCETTA and VEGETABLES

· **Creamy Gnocchi Soup:** *Sauté a little butter and flour in a pot to make a roux, then whisk in chicken stock and some heavy cream to create a souplike consistency. Add leftover gnocchi, pancetta, and veggies and simmer until heated through. Taste and adjust the seasoning, if desired. Garnish with Parmesan cheese.*

· **Gnocchi Hash:** *Crisp leftovers in a skillet and top with a fried egg for a hearty breakfast hash.*

· **Gnocchi-Stuffed Peppers:** *Mix leftover gnocchi, pancetta, and veggies with a bit of ricotta or cream cheese. Stuff the mixture into halved and seeded bell peppers and sprinkle with Parmesan. Bake at 375°F until the peppers are tender and the filling is hot and bubbly, about 20 minutes.*

· **Pasta Salad:** *Toss cold leftovers with cooked and cooled pasta of choice, then add a little extra balsamic and fresh greens for texture.*

HERBED BUTTER SPATCHCOCKED CHICKEN

· **Chicken and Veggie Panini:** *Layer shredded leftover chicken, leftover roasted vegetables, provolone cheese, and a smear of grainy mustard or garlic aioli on crusty bread. Grill in a panini press or skillet until golden and melty.*

· **Herbed Chicken Pot Pie:** *Sauté a little butter and flour in a pot to make a roux, then whisk in about 1 cup chicken stock and a splash of heavy cream. Mix in 1½ cups shredded leftover chicken and leftover roasted vegetables. Pour the filling into a baking dish and top with puff pastry or biscuit dough. Bake at 350°F until the pastry is golden brown and the filling is heated through, 25 to 30 minutes.*

JAMBALAYA

· **Jambalaya Burrito Bowl:** *Layer leftover jambalaya in a bowl with sliced avocado, pico de gallo, shredded lettuce, sour cream, cilantro, and a squeeze of lime.*

· **Jambalaya Omelet:** *Add leftover jambalaya to a fluffy omelet with shredded cheddar or pepper jack cheese.*

· **Jambalaya Soup:** *Thin the leftovers with chicken stock to transform it into a hearty soup.*

· **Jambalaya-Stuffed Peppers:** *Cut bell peppers in half, remove the seeds, and stuff with leftover jambalaya. Top with shredded mozzarella cheese and bake at 375°F until warmed through, browned, and bubbly, about 20 minutes.*

LEMON-DILL CHICKEN with ARTICHOKES

· **Chicken and Artichoke Risotto:** *Stir chopped leftover chicken and artichokes into a creamy risotto near the end of cooking. Add a splash of lemon juice, fresh dill, and Parmesan.*

· **Creamy Lemon Chicken Pasta:** *Slice leftover chicken and chop the artichokes. Toss into cooked pasta with a splash of the pasta water to thin the creamy sauce. Top with extra Parmesan, fresh dill, and a squeeze of lemon for a bright finish.*

LEMON-HERB ROASTED CHICKEN

· **Chicken and Rice Casserole:** *Mix chopped leftover chicken with cooked rice, a creamy sauce like Alfredo or cream of chicken soup, and some vegetables. Top with cheese and bake until bubbly and golden.*

· **Chicken Salad:** *Mix shredded leftover chicken with mayo, Dijon mustard, cubed avocado, celery, green onions, dill, salt, and pepper.*

· *See also* **Chicken Pot Pie Pizza**, *page 328.*

MUFFULETTA CHICKEN

· **Grilled Muffuletta Sandwich:** *Chop up leftover meats and cheese and pile onto sourdough or focaccia along with Olive Salad (page 308) and some extra cheese. Press in a panini press or grill in a skillet until golden and melty.*

· **Muffuletta Chicken Caesar Salad:** *Chop up the leftover chicken, meats, cheeses, and olive salad and add it to a Kale, Spinach, and Romaine Caesar (page 207). Top with Crispy Garlic Chickpeas (page 84).*

· **Muffuletta Chicken Omelet:** *Dice the leftover chicken, meats, and cheeses and layer with olive salad in a fluffy omelet. Serve with crusty bread for a savory, Mediterranean-inspired brunch.*

· **Muffuletta Pasta:** *Slice the meats and cheeses and serve over cooked pasta with a drizzle of olive oil and a few spoonfuls of olive salad for a quick, Mediterranean-inspired pasta.*

PULLED PORK

· **Pulled Pork Pizza:** *Spread BBQ sauce on a pizza crust, then top with leftover pulled pork, red onions, cilantro, and cheese. Bake at 350°F until the crust is golden brown and the cheese is bubbly.*

· **Pulled Pork Sandwiches:** *Pile leftover pulled pork on toasted buns with your favorite BBQ sauce, coleslaw, and pickles.*

· *See also* **Pulled Pork–Stuffed Sweet Potatoes**, *page 322.*

PORK CHOPS with LEMON-THYME PAN SAUCE

· **Breakfast Skillet:** *Chop leftover pork into small pieces and heat up in a skillet with potatoes, peppers, and onions, then top with a fried egg.*

· **Pork Grain Bowl:** *Spoon leftover chopped pork and roasted vegetables over cooked rice or quinoa and drizzle with leftover pan sauce.*

· **Pork Sandwich:** *Layer leftover pork in a crusty roll with caramelized onions, arugula, and some Dijon mustard.*

· **Pork and Spinach Pasta:** *Toss leftover pork and pan sauce with cooked pasta, a handful of spinach, and some grated Parmesan cheese.*

REUBEN EGG ROLLS

· **Reuben Egg Roll Grilled Cheese:** *Butter two slices of bread and layer with shredded Swiss and Gruyère cheeses, then add chopped leftover Reuben egg rolls. Grill the sandwich over medium heat for 4 to 5 minutes per side, until crispy and golden. Slice and serve with Russian dressing for dipping.*

· **Reuben Egg Roll Lettuce Wraps:** *Use large lettuce leaves (like butter lettuce or Romaine) to wrap chopped up leftover egg rolls. Top with extra pickles and a drizzle of Russian dressing*

· **Reuben Egg Roll Omelet:** *Chop up leftover egg rolls and use them as a filling for an omelet. Add a little extra Swiss cheese and a drizzle of Russian dressing. Garnish with chopped fresh chives.*

ROASTED BLACKENED CHICKEN and VEGETABLES

· **Blackened Chicken and Veggie Pasta:** *Cut leftover chicken and roasted vegetables into bite-sized pieces. Toss with cooked pasta, olive oil, garlic, and Parmesan cheese.*

· **Blackened Chicken and Veggie Quesadillas:** *Layer chopped leftover chicken and roasted vegetables with shredded pepper jack cheese inside tortillas. Grill until crispy and golden. Serve with Avocado Ranch Dressing (page 304).*

ROASTED SALMON and VEGETABLES

· **Salmon Niçoise Salad:** *Combine flaked leftover salmon and leftover roasted vegetables with hard-boiled eggs, boiled baby potatoes, olives, egg, and fresh greens. Drizzle with a classic Dijon vinaigrette (olive oil, Dijon mustard, and red wine vinegar). Serve with lemon wedges.*

· **Salmon and Veggie Fried Rice:** *Flake leftover salmon and chop leftover roasted vegetables into small pieces. Sauté them in a hot skillet with garlic, ginger, and a bit of sesame oil. Add cooked rice, a splash of soy sauce, and a scrambled egg. Finish with fresh dill or green onions.*

SPICE-RUBBED PORK TENDERLOIN

· **Pork Tenderloin Banh Mi:** *Layer thinly sliced leftover pork in a baguette with pickled carrots, cucumbers, cilantro, and a spicy mayonnaise or sriracha.*

· **Pork Tenderloin Potstickers:** *Combine finely chopped leftover pork with cabbage, ginger, garlic, and soy sauce. Use as a filling for homemade potstickers or dumplings, pan-frying them for a crispy bottom and steamed top.*

SWEDISH MEATBALLS

· **Meatball Casserole:** *Layer leftover meatballs with cooked pasta or rice and sauce, then top with the shredded cheese of choice. Bake at 300°F until bubbly and warmed through, about 20 minutes.*

· **Meatball Sandwiches:** *Pile leftover meatballs on a hoagie bun, drizzle with some of the sauce, and top with the cheese of choice and sautéed onions and mushrooms.*

TERIYAKI CHICKEN

· **Teriyaki Chicken Stir-Fry:** *Sauté leftover chicken with stir-fry vegetables like bell peppers, broccoli, and snap peas. Add a little extra soy sauce and serve over rice or noodles.*

· **Teriyaki Chicken Wraps:** *Wrap leftover chicken in a lettuce or cabbage leaf with rice, avocado, carrots, and bell peppers. Drizzle with leftover sauce and roll up.*

ALLERGEN AND DIETARY INDEX

RECIPES	PAGE	🌾	🥛	⊘	⊘	🌿	LOW CARB
Muffuletta Chicken	63	✓		✓	✓		✓
Herbed Butter Spatchcocked Chicken	64	✓		✓	✓		
Roasted Blackened Chicken and Vegetables	66	✓	✓	✓	✓		✓
Roasted Salmon and Vegetables	68	✓	✓	✓	✓		✓
Crab and Shrimp–Stuffed Salmon with Caper-Dill Hollandaise	71			✓			✓
Chicken Tacos	72	✓		✓			✓
Gnocchi with Pancetta and Vegetables	75			✓			
Cuban Potato Skins	76	✓		✓	✓		
Upside-Down Caramelized Shallot and Brie Tarts	79			✓		✓	
Baked Heirloom Caprese with Warm Bacon Vinaigrette	80	✓		✓	✓		✓
Cheesy Garlic Roasted Asparagus	83	✓		✓	✓		✓
Crispy Garlic Chickpeas	84	✓	✓	✓	✓	✓	✓
Garlic Butter Steak Bites	95	✓		✓	✓		✓
Balsamic Pesto Beef Kabobs	96	✓			✓		✓
Chili-Lime Flank Steak with Grilled Corn Salsa	98	✓		✓	✓		
Sloppy Macs	100			✓			
Copycat Hamburger Helper Beef Stroganoff	103			✓	✓		
Reuben Egg Rolls	104			✓			
Egg Roll Burgers	107			✓			
Parmesan-Crusted Chicken with Lemon Cream Sauce	108	✓		✓			✓
Crispy Chicken Thigh Piccata	111	✓		✓	✓		✓
Lemon-Dill Chicken with Artichokes	112	✓		✓	✓		✓
Blackened Mahi Mahi with Pineapple Salsa	115	✓	✓	✓	✓		
Cheesy Spinach-Stuffed Peppers	116	✓		✓	✓	✓	✓
Simple Grilled Vegetables	119	✓	✓	✓	✓	✓	
Creamy Dill Egg Salad	120	✓	✓	✓		✓	✓
Bacon and Gruyère Egg Bites	122	✓		✓			✓
Baked Ham and Egg Skillet	124	✓		✓			✓
Freezer Breakfast Sandwiches	127			✓			
Jambalaya	137			✓	✓		
Beef Birria	138	✓	✓	✓	✓		✓
Pork Chops with Lemon-Thyme Pan Sauce	141	✓		✓	✓		✓
Cabbage Roll in a Bowl	142	✓	✓	✓	✓		✓
Lemon-Herb Roasted Chicken	145	✓		✓	✓		
French Onion Chicken	146	✓		✓	✓		✓
Creamy Chicken Marsala	149			✓	✓		
Chicken Scallopini with Tomatoes	150	✓		✓	✓		✓

RECIPES	PAGE	🌾	🥛	🥜	🥚	🌱	LOW CARB
Creamy Garlic Scallops Piccata	153	✓		✓	✓		✓
Pesto Steamed Clams	154	✓			✓		✓
Philly Cheesesteak French Onion Soup	157			✓	✓		
Roasted Red Pepper, Tomato, and Smoked Gouda Bisque	158	✓		✓	✓	✓	✓
Dill Pickle Soup	161			✓	✓	✓	
Steamed Artichokes	162	✓	✓	✓	✓	✓	✓
Dutch Oven Ranch Popcorn	165			✓	✓	✓	
Balsamic Short Ribs	172	✓	✓	✓	✓		
Mississippi Pot Roast	174			✓	✓		✓
Swedish Meatballs	177			✓			
Kickin' Chili	178	✓		✓	✓		✓
Pulled Pork	181	✓		✓	✓		✓
Pork Chops with Carrots and Mushrooms	182			✓	✓		
Teriyaki Chicken	185	✓	✓	✓	✓		
Lentil and Italian Sausage Soup	186	✓		✓	✓		
Garlic-Herb Mashed Potatoes	189	✓		✓	✓	✓	
Pancake Board	196						
Bagel Board	198			✓			
Wedge Spread	200	✓					✓
Chili Charcuterie	202			✓	✓		
Burger Board	204			✓			
Kale, Spinach, and Romaine Caesar	207	✓		✓			✓
Chimichurri Chicken Salad Bowls	208	✓		✓	✓		✓
California Roll in a Bowl	211		✓	✓			
Greek Salmon Bowls	212	✓		✓			✓
Umami Beef Bowls	215	✓	✓	✓	✓		
Hoisin Beef Bowls	216		✓		✓		
Cherry Ricotta Toast	225			✓	✓	✓	
Benedict Toast with Caramelized Onions	226			✓			
Green Eggs and Ham on Toast	229						
Pizza Eggs on Toast	230			✓			
Caesar Salad Breakfast Toast	233			✓			
Dill Egg Salad Toast	234			✓		✓	
Smoked Salmon Toast	237			✓			
Chili Crisp Avocado Toast	238						
Black Forest Ham and Feta Avocado Toast	241			✓			
Tomato Confit Toast	242					✓	

RECIPES	PAGE	🌾	🥛	⊘	⊘	🍃	LOW CARB
Salmon and Cilantro-Lime Slaw	251	✓		✓			✓
Tuna Melt Fritters	252			✓			✓
Garlic Parmesan Chicken Skewers	255	✓		✓	✓		✓
Spice-Rubbed Pork Tenderloin	256	✓	✓	✓	✓		✓
Umami Brussels Sprouts	259	✓	✓	✓	✓	✓	✓
Furikake Potato Wedges	260	✓	✓	✓		✓	
Loaded Greek Fries	263	✓		✓	✓	✓	
Pasta Chips	264			✓	✓	✓	
Apple Hand Pies	267			✓		✓	
Brûlée Bananas	268	✓			✓	✓	
Biscuits and Gravy Casserole	277			✓			
Ham and Cheese Croissant Casserole	278			✓			
French Toast Casserole	281					✓	
Caramelized Onion and Prosciutto Mac and Cheese	282			✓			
Tuscan Chicken Pasta	285			✓	✓		
Mushroom Orzo with Crispy Prosciutto and Sage	286			✓			
Carbonara Frittata	289			✓			
Creamy Taco Pasta	290			✓			
Italian Grinder Pasta Salad	293			✓			
Street Corn Pasta Salad	294			✓		✓	
Cilantro-Lime Avocado Dressing	300	✓		✓		✓	✓
Lemon-Caper Aioli	301	✓	✓	✓		✓	✓
Caper-Dill Hollandaise	303	✓		✓		✓	✓
Avocado Ranch Dressing	304	✓		✓		✓	✓
Russian Dressing	304	✓	✓	✓		✓	✓
Caesar Dressing	305	✓		✓		✓	✓
Burger Sauce	305	✓	✓	✓		✓	✓
Yum Yum Sauce	306	✓	✓	✓		✓	✓
Cucumber Sauce	307	✓		✓		✓	✓
Olive Salad	308	✓	✓	✓	✓	✓	✓
Roasted Garlic Two Ways	310	✓	✓	✓	✓	✓	✓
Tomato Confit	312	✓	✓	✓	✓	✓	✓
Herby Everything Seasoning	314	✓	✓	✓	✓	✓	✓
Blackened Seasoning	315	✓	✓	✓	✓	✓	✓
Taco Seasoning	315	✓	✓	✓	✓	✓	✓
Quesabirria Tacos	321			✓	✓		
Pulled Pork–Stuffed Sweet Potatoes	322	✓		✓	✓		
Flank Steak Tacos	325			✓	✓		
Chili Cheese Egg Muffins	326	✓		✓			
Chicken Pot Pie Pizza	328			✓			
Mississippi Pot Roast Grilled Cheese	330			✓	✓		

GENERAL INDEX